Bernard Lewis, a world-respected authority on Islamic and Middle Eastern history, is Emeritus Professor of Near Eastern Studies at Princeton University, where he has been since 1974. Born in London in 1916, he was Professor of the History of the Middle East at the School of Oriental and African Studies, University of London, 1949–74. He is the author of many books, which have been translated into over twenty languages, including Arabic, Persian, Turkish, Malay and Indonesian.

The Multiple Identities of the Middle East

Bernard Lewis

PHŒNIX

A Phoenix Paperback
First published in Great Britain by Weidenfeld & Nicolson in 1998
This paperback edition published in 1999 by Phoenix,
an imprint of Orion Books Ltd,
Orion House, 5 Upper St Martin's Lane,
London WC2H 9EA

A CIP catalogue record for this book
is available from the British Library.

ISBN: 0 75380 874 9

Printed in Great Britain by
The Guernsey Press Co. Ltd, Guernsey, C. I.

To Buntzie, a gift

≡CONTENTS

MAPS

=PREFACE

The nucleus of this book was three papers, submitted to conferences held in Wolfenbüttel (1989), Rome (1993), and Castelgandolfo (1995). These papers were published in the conference proceedings. In expanding and recasting them for this book, I have also drawn on some other lectures, articles, and conference papers. My thanks are due to the conveners and editors who persuaded me to take up this subject, and to the participants, whose comments and questions helped me to refine and improve my perceptions of these matters.

Once again, I would like to express my thanks to my assistant, Annamarie Cerminaro, who with her usual combination of skill and patience nursed my manuscript from first draft to final published text. I should also like to thank Robin Pettinato who helped her greatly in this process.

Finally, a word of thanks to two friends who were kind enough to read my draft – Buntzie Churchill and Michael Curtis. I offer them my thanks for those suggestions and improvements which I accepted; my apologies for those that I resisted. From this it will be clear that any faults that remain are entirely my own.

⹀INTRODUCTION

The title of this book, as the reader will recognize, is borrowed from the language of psychology or, to be more precise, of psychiatry. In using this title I do not mean to suggest that the Middle East is suffering from morbid psychological problems. Still less is it my intention to offer any kind of therapy.

What I want to convey by this title is something of the complexity and variety of the different identities which can be held at one and the same time by groups, even more than by individuals – the constant change and evolution of identity in the Middle East, of the ways in which the peoples of the region perceive themselves, the groups to which they belong, and the difference between self and other.

Even in the Western world there are multiple identities. Since the foundation of the United Kingdom, every one of its people has had at least three identities: by nationality, as a British subject, later as a U.K. citizen; by what we nowadays call ethnicity, as a member of one or more of the four indigenous components of that nationality, the English, Scots, Welsh and Irish; and by religion. In modern times, the range of both ethnicity and religion, within the common British nationality, has been greatly widened, and the subgroups are increasingly mixed. They are even more mixed in the United States, where, similarly, every citizen, in addition to his U.S. citizenship, has other identities, defined by race, by ethnic origin or, often, origins, and by his personal or ancestral religion.

Like America, Russia too embraces many ethnic groups, acquired not by immigration but by conquest and annexation. France and Spain both have important regional minorities; some of them, like the Bretons and the Basques, preserve languages that are totally different from the official national language. But these are old-established and indigenous, and show no significant cultural or religious differences from the dominant majorities. Elsewhere in Europe ethnic minorities have hitherto been small, few, and without legal or political status or even claims.

This situation has now changed dramatically, as the immigration of millions of newcomers has created new minorities. These are numerous, widely dispersed, and differ ethnically, linguistically, culturally, religiously, and often even racially from the majority indigenous population. Naturally, they bring with them their own concepts and perceptions of identity, which may differ significantly from those of Europe and the West. Both terms, 'Europe' and 'West', are of course European and Western, and until the nineteenth century had little or no meaning in other parts of the world, notably in the Middle East. The same is true of the names 'Asia' and 'Africa'.

Europe is a European idea, conceived in Greece, nurtured in Rome, and now, after a long and troubled childhood and adolescence in Christendom, approaching maturity in a secular, supranational community. Asia and Africa are also European ideas, European ways of describing the Other. All human groups have terms, often derogatory, to designate those who are outside the group. Some of these terms have acquired an almost universal significance. Barbarians were originally non-Greeks, gentiles are non-Jews; Asians and Africans are non-Europeans, and their continents mark the boundaries of Europe, as perceived by Europeans, in the east and the south.

During the long struggle between Christendom and Islam, these boundaries changed many times. Barbarians did not, of course, regard themselves as barbarians, nor did gentiles regard themselves as gentiles until both were taught, by the processes of Hellenization and Christianization, to see themselves in this alien light. The Hellenization of the barbarians took place in antiquity; the Christianization of the gentiles in the Middle Ages. The awareness among Asians and Africans of this European-defined identity dates, in the main, from modern times, when they were taught this classification by European rulers, teachers and preachers. By the present day, the Greek invention of the three continents of the Old World has been universally accepted. The enterprise and ingenuity of mostly European explorers and geographers have added several more.

'Middle East' is self-evidently a Western term, and dates from the beginning of this century. It is a striking testimony to the former power and continuing influence of the West that this parochial term, meaningful only in a Western perspective, has come to be used all over the world. It is even used by the peoples of the region it denotes to describe their own homelands. This is the more remarkable in an age of national, communal, and regional self-assertion, mostly in anti-Western form.

Within every society there are multiple identities, each with variations and with sometimes conflicting subdivisions. These identities may be social and economic – by status, class, occupation and profession. Generation and gender provide two major demarcations of identity; so too do such contrasts as civil and military, lay and ecclesiastical, and the like. In the Bible (Genesis 4), the story of the first clash and the first murder is told against a background of socio-economic rivalry. 'Abel was a keeper of sheep, but Cain was a tiller of the ground.' Both brought offerings to God, the one 'of the fruit of the ground', the other 'of the firstlings of his flock'. God preferred the second, and Cain, in anger and envy 'rose up against Abel his brother, and slew him'. The rivalry between nomadic herdsmen and peasant cultivators is a recurring theme throughout Middle Eastern history, and in many parts of the region the clash of interests between the two remains important at the present day. In Genesis, the peasant kills the nomad; more often in Middle Eastern history it has been the other way around. Later, with the growth of cities, a more sophisticated clash of identities and loyalties arose, between the city and the countryside, and between quarters in the city, often combining ethnic, communal, and occupational identities. In the larger empires, like those of the Caliphs, regional identities and loyalties could acquire social and cultural, but rarely political importance.

Social and economic conflicts have an obvious importance in the development of identities and loyalties within a society. With few exceptions, they have had little or no effect on the realities or even, until very recently, on the perception of differences between societies. The one great attempt at a supranational identity and solidarity based on the working class foundered on the rocks of Russian nationalism and Soviet state interest.

Gender differences obviously have immense social and cultural influence on the evolution of attitudes and identities in any society; in the male-dominated Middle East they are only now beginning to have political impact.

In the Middle East as elsewhere, historical and literary records show that it was not by social or economic, nor yet by generational and gender differences, that people saw the basic definition of their own identity, the dividing line between self and other. These were – or have hitherto been – determined by more traditional criteria.

The primary identities are those acquired at birth. These are of three kinds. The first is by blood, that is to say, in ascending order, the family, the clan, the tribe, developing into the ethnic nation. The second is by place, often but not necessarily coinciding with the first and sometimes indeed in conflict with it. This may mean the village or neighbourhood, district or quarter, province or city, developing in modern times into the country. The third, often linked with the first or second, or both, is the religious community, which may be subdivided into sects. For many, religion is the only loyalty that transcends local and immediate bonds.

The second broad category of identity is that of allegiance

to a ruler, in the past usually a hereditary monarch. This identity is normally acquired by birth. It may be changed by annexation, by transfer of power, or, for the individual, by migration, and, in modern times, naturalization. It is expressed in the obedience owed by the subject to the sovereign and to his multifarious representatives at the various levels at which a subject lives his life – the head of the state or of a department, the governor of a province or city, the administrator of a district, the headman of a village.

In most of the world, and for most of the history of the Middle East, these two identities – the involuntary identity of birth and the compulsory identity of the state – were the only ones that existed. In modern times, under the influence of the West, a new kind is evolving between the two – the freely chosen cohesion and loyalty of voluntary associations, combining to form what is nowadays known as the civil society.

ONE

Definitions

The Middle East is a region of old and deep-rooted identities, which in modern times have undergone crucial changes. The study and even the perception of these identities is rendered more complicated and difficult by the fact that we – and to a growing extent, even the peoples of the Middle East – perceive them, discuss them, even think about them, in language borrowed from another society with different systems of group identity. I am writing this in English, a Western language, but the same problem would arise if I were writing in Arabic or any other language in use in the Middle East today. The language of modern political discourse in the region is Western, even if local words are used. Some of these words, like democracy or dictatorship, are loanwords or neologisms devised to render Western terms; others, like government or freedom, are old words, injected with new meanings. This is true of much of the language of public debate in the Middle East at the present time. It is particularly true of the current language of political identity and allegiance, which is derived primarily from the historical experience of Europe.

But the old realities do not disappear. In clashes with the alien outsider, however perceived and defined; in struggles between rival groups or rival identities within the society, new words are sometimes used with old meanings, and old words retain or resume their original content.

It may therefore be useful to take another look at these various terms, and to try and redefine them in a sense that is more in accord with both the legacy of the Middle Eastern past and the realities of the Middle Eastern present. Nationality and citizenship, nationalism and patriotism are new words in the Middle East, devised to denote new notions. Nation, people, country, community and state are old words, but they are words of unstable and therefore explosive content. To complicate matters further, the same may be true even of the names of specific ethnic, national, communal, and territorial entities.

In January 1923, as part of the final settling of accounts between the various successor states of the Ottoman Empire and the victorious Allies, a convention and protocol were agreed and signed between the governments of Greece and Turkey, providing for a compulsory exchange of minorities between the two countries. Two regions were exempted – the city of Istanbul in Turkey and the province of western Thrace in Greece. Elsewhere, the minorities had no choice but, by the agreement of the two governments, to leave their homes and be resettled in the country of their presumed identity. The first article of the agreement further specified that no person thus transferred was permitted to return to his previous home – neither to Turkey without the permission of the Turkish government, nor to Greece without the permission of the Greek government.

The matter was clearly seen as urgent. The Lausanne Protocol was dated 30 January 1923; the transfers were to begin on 1 May of the same year. Between 1923 and 1930, an estimated million and a quarter Greeks were sent from Turkey to Greece and a somewhat smaller number of Turks from Greece to Turkey. At least, that is how they are described in almost all accounts of this exchange. That is not, however, how they are described in the protocol, which speaks of the persons to be exchanged as 'Turkish subjects of the Greek orthodox religion residing in Turkey' and 'Greek subjects of the Muslim religion residing in Greece'.

A closer look at what actually happened, at the hundreds of thousands of so-called Greeks and Turks who were 'repatriated', confirms the accuracy with which the phrasing of the protocol reflects the perceptions and intentions of those who drafted and signed it. A visitor to the Anatolian Turkish province of Karaman, from which many Greeks were sent to Greece, will find traces of their past presence – churches and cemeteries with inscriptions in Greek characters. But a closer look will reveal that while the script is Greek, the language is often Turkish. The Karamanian 'Greeks' were indeed Greek in the sense that they were adherents of the Greek Orthodox Church, but the language they used, among themselves as well as with others, was Turkish – which, however, they wrote in the Greek script and not in the Arabic script used by their Muslim neighbours. That script was, of course, used by their counterparts who came from Greece, by the Greek-speaking Muslim minority from Crete and other places in Greece, most of whom knew little or no Turkish, but spoke Greek and sometimes wrote it in the Turco-Arabic script.

This association of script and religion – to be precise, of script and scripture, was the common pattern in the Middle East. For more than a thousand years, from the Arabization to the modernization of Syria, Christians, Muslims and Jews in that country spoke and wrote Arabic, but Muslims wrote it in the Arabic script, Christians in the Syriac script and Jews in the Hebrew script, each community using the form of writing that was sanctified by its holy book and required for its worship. The clergy and, more generally, the learned, usually knew the language as well as the script of the holy books, but for most ordinary people, the script was enough, and they used it to write their vernaculars. Apart from a small educated elite, the Karamanian Greeks did not learn Greek until they arrived in Greece; the Cretan Turks did not learn Turkish until they were resettled in Turkey. On both sides there were problems of acculturation and assimilation.

A Western observer, accustomed to a different system of classification, might well conclude that what was agreed and accomplished by the governments of Greece and Turkey was not an exchange and repatriation of ethnic or national minorities, but rather two deportations into exile of religious minorities – of Muslim Greeks to Turkey, of Christian Turks to Greece.

Even the terms used – Greeks and Turks, Greece and Turkey – present some mysteries. The word used by the Turks, and more generally by Muslims in the Middle East, to designate the Greeks is *Rūm*. But *Rūm* doesn't mean Greeks; *Rūm* means Romans, and the use of the name, first by the Greeks themselves and then by their new Muslim masters, echoes their last memory of political sovereignty and greatness – the Byzantine Empire. 'Byzantine' is of course a term of modern scholarship. The Byzantines never called themselves Byzantines, any more than the ancient Britons or Anglo-Saxons called themselves ancient Britons or Anglo-Saxons. For its rulers and people, the state that was finally extinguished in 1453 was the Roman Empire. Its capital was in Constantinople not Rome; its language was Greek not Latin. But it was the legitimate heir of Imperial Rome, and its people called themselves Romans, albeit in Greek. For the Ottomans, the name *Rūm* denoted the East Roman Empire which they had conquered and superseded – the empire in which Greek was the official language and Greek Orthodoxy was the established church. Because of this, under Ottoman rule, the *Rūm* ranked first among the non-Muslim communities (*millet*). Westerners, haunted by the memories of a more ancient past, called that community Greek or later, in a neo-classical mood, Hellenic; but for both Christians and Muslims in the Empire it was still Roman and in a sense even imperial, including Orthodox

Serbs, Bulgars, Albanians, and Arabs as well as ethnic Greeks. The rising nationalist movements among the Balkan peoples in the nineteenth century fought a battle on two fronts, seeking at the same time to overthrow both the ascendancy of the ethnic Greeks within their church, and the domination of the Ottoman Turks over their homelands.

The term 'Ottoman Turks' raises similar difficulties. The official language of the Ottoman Empire was usually described as Turkish, but the people did not call themselves Turks, nor did they call their country Turkey. The words Turk and Turkey had been used in Europe at least since the twelfth century, but they were not used by Turks in Turkey. Instead these designated the country they ruled in religious terms, as the lands of Islam; in dynastic terms, as the Ottoman realms; or, when a more precise territorial definition was needed, by the name inherited from their predecessors in empire – the land of *Rūm*. 'Turkey' was not officially adopted as the name of the country until after the establishment of the Republic in 1923. Even in Europe, the word 'Turk' had a primarily religious connotation. It included Ottoman and sometimes even other Muslims of many different ethnic and language groups. It did not include Christian or Jewish inhabitants of the Ottoman realm, even if – as happened in some regions – they spoke Turkish. In contrast, a European convert to Islam was said to have 'turned Turk' even if the conversion took place in Iran or Morocco.

In general, religious and ethnic terms were commonly confused on both the Christian and Muslim shores of the Mediterranean. Both were unwilling to apply explicitly religious terms to the other, and thus admit the fact of a rival universal religion. For a long time, European Christians did not use religious designations like 'Muslim' or 'Islam'. Sometimes they used the inaccurate and misleading term Muhammadan, coined by analogy with Christian. More often, they designated the Muslims by ethnic terms such as Moor, Saracen, Turk, and Tatar. Muslim writers in pre-modern times show a similar disinclination to use the religious term Christian, and preferred to describe the peoples of Europe either by the vague general term 'unbelievers', or, more commonly, by such ethnic terms as Roman, Frank, and Slav. All three, again, have in Muslim usage a religious more than an ethnic connotation, and denote an identity that can be acquired or relinquished by religious conversion. When a specifically religious designation for Christians was needed, they were usually called *Nasrānī* (plural *Nasārā*), Nazarenes, i.e. followers of Jesus of Nazareth. In Ottoman protocol and in modern Arabic usage the term *masīhī*, a literal translation of 'Christian' (from Arabic *masīh* = Hebrew messiah = Greek *Khristos*, anointed) is the polite name.

The relative importance of religion and country in the traditional Muslim view of the world may be seen in the heading of the letters sent to Queen Elizabeth by a Muslim ruler, the Ottoman Sultan Murad III. These letters all begin with the following titles:

> Pride of the virtuous matrons of the followers of Jesus, elder of the honoured ladies of the Christian community, moderator of the affairs of the Nazarene sect, who draws the trains of nobility and dignity, mistress of the tokens of grandeur and glory, queen of the land of England, may her life end well.

The Queen, it will be noted, is defined in the first, second and third places as a Christian leader, and only in the fourth place as ruler of a territory called England. Some documents are more specific, and define her as a leader of the 'Lutheran' Christians. The Turkish word translated as 'land' in these titles is *vilâyet*, with the connotation of a province or administrative area, rather than a country in the modern sense. The Turkish terms for 'king' and 'queen' are of European origin, and are never in any circumstances applied to Turkish or other Muslim monarchs. Their use in Turkish documents for European Christian rulers exactly parallels the use of native titles for native princes in British India. Not surprisingly, it became a point of honour among European monarchs to demand that the sultans accord them the same titles – and thus status – as they claimed for themselves. As the Ottomans grew weaker and the European powers grew stronger, one European monarch after another demanded that he or she be addressed, in Ottoman documents, by the sultan's own title of *padishah*.

The modern, secularized Westerner has great difficulty in understanding a culture in which not nationality, not citizenship, not descent, but religion, or more precisely membership of a religious community, is the ultimate determinant of identity. For more than a hundred years, much of the Middle East has been under the spell of Europe – first influence, then dominance, and then, when dominance ended, influence again. During this time, Western ideas of national self-determination have profoundly affected all its peoples, Muslim and other. But even today, the old communal solidarities and allegiances are always a powerful and sometimes a determining factor. This can be seen not only in Muslim countries but also in other countries which were for a long time part of the Ottoman Empire and have retained, even after their independence, many traces of Ottoman perceptions and practices.

Two recent examples may suffice. One of them comes from Greece, now a member of the European Union, within which citizens of member states may travel freely, using identity cards and not needing passports. The Greek government clashed with the European authority in Brussels because of the line for religion on Greek identity cards. No other European country has such an entry, and this was regarded as contrary to European democratic practice. But the Greeks insisted, arguing that religion is an essential part of their identity.

A more serious and more tragic example may be seen in

the former Yugoslavia. Ottoman rule never extended to the whole of that country, and ended by the early years of this century. Yet the recent and current conflicts among Yugoslavs are in a very real sense a continuation of the bitter struggles that marked the death throes of the Ottoman Empire. Western observers and commentators usually describe the complex relations between Serbs, Croats and Muslims in national terms and speak of ethnic conflicts and ethnic cleansing. In the days when Yugoslavia was ruled by a Communist, Marxist dictatorship, religion had no place in the political taxonomy of the country. But even the Communist regime was obliged to recognize the separate identity of the Muslims. They did so by distinguishing between muslim, with a lower case m, which denoted a religion, and Muslim, with a capital m, which denoted a recognized 'nationality' among those forming the Yugoslav federation.

Considering what was done and said in Bosnia, one may wonder whether such terms as 'national' and 'ethnic' have much relevance. Ethnically, the three major groups, the Serbs, Croats and Muslims, are much the same. The language they use is also much the same, though in accordance with old Middle Eastern practice, it is written by Orthodox Serbs in the Cyrillic script, by Catholic Croats in the Latin script and was written by Muslim Bosniaks, until the present century, in the Arabic script. The same kind of confusion and conflict, arising from the overlapping yet contrasting identities of citizenship, community and ethnicity, can be seen in one form or another in many Middle Eastern countries.

The modern Western observer, even in countries where the separation of church and state is not part of the law, no longer attaches primary importance to religious identity; he therefore has difficulty in grasping that others may still do so, and will tend to see – or seek – a non-religious explanation for ostensibly religious conflicts. There are, of course, exceptions in the West, some of them obvious, such as the conflict between Protestants and Catholics in Northern Ireland. But even this is usually portrayed, chiefly by non-participants, in national rather than religious terms, as a simple conflict between British and Irish. Western reporters trying to make the complexities of the Lebanese civil wars intelligible to their Western readers fell into the habit of speaking of 'right-wing Christians' in conflict with 'left-wing Muslims' – as if the seating arrangements of the revolutionary French National Assembly of 1789 were of any relevance to the sectarian struggles by which Lebanon was riven apart. Certainly such Western terminology cannot describe, still less explain a conflict in which, in most domestic situations, the rival factions would define themselves as Catholic or Orthodox rather than Christian, Sunni or Shī'a rather than Muslim, and any of these rather than Lebanese.

In the Lausanne Protocol of 1923, the individuals to be transferred are identified according to two categories – as adherents of a religion, and as subjects of a state. In the Middle East the first of these is old established and universally understood and accepted; the second, in its present form at least, is new. In the Western world, documents of identity issued for purposes of travel used to define their holders as subjects of this or that monarch, or, later, as citizens of this or that republic. In modern times the term citizen has replaced subject even in the surviving monarchies. Both terms indicate the state to which the individual owes allegiance and, within variously defined limits, obedience, and from which he receives protection in return.

A number of terms are used to denote this relationship. In English, both British and American, the word commonly used is 'nationality' which basically means what is written on a passport. *Nationalité* in French and the equivalents in some other European languages are used in much the same way. But not in all. German *Nationalität* and Russian *natsional'nost* convey ethnic and cultural, not legal and political nationality. For these they use other words – *Staatsangehörigkeit*, 'state-belonging' in German, *graždanstvo* 'citizenship' in Russian. English legal usage still has no accepted term to denote this kind of ethnic, cultural identity within a nationality. Half a century ago it was still common practice to refer to the four components of British nationality, the English, the Scots, the Welsh, and the Irish, as 'races', but changes in the content and impact of this word have made such usage unacceptable. Even within Europe, there are thus significant variations of terminology and usage. Variation – and the opportunity for confusion – becomes greater in regions where this whole terminology was sometimes borrowed, sometimes imposed, but remained alien to a large part of the population.

The commonest modern Western word denoting political identity and allegiance is of course citizenship. Curiously, Middle Eastern languages have, or until recently had, no words for citizen or for citizenship. The modern Persian term, *shahrvand*, from *shahr*, city, is an obvious loan translation. The words commonly used as equivalent of citizen, *muwātin* in Arabic, *vatandaş* or *yurttaş* in Turkish, *hamvatan* in Persian, have the literal meaning of compatriot, one from the same *watan* or country. Modern Hebrew follows a similiar course, using *ezrah* and *ezrahūt* for citizen and citizenship. *Ezrahut* is new. *Ezrah* occurs a number of times in Exodus (12:19, 48, 49), Leviticus (16:29; 17:15; 18:26; 19:34; 24:16, 22) and Numbers (9:14; 15:13–15, 29, 30), where it is normally contrasted with *gēr*, the stranger or 'sojourner in your midst'. *Ezrah* is usually translated in the Authorized Version as 'one of your own country' or, sometimes, 'your own nation'. Other variants are 'one born amongst you' and 'one born in the land'. The point of these passages, it may be noted in passing, is to insist that the stranger or sojourner be accorded the same treatment as the home-born, without discrimination.

The common term, in classical Islamic usage, for the subjects of the State was *ra'iyya*, literally flocks or herds, an expression of the pastoral image of government common to the three Middle Eastern religions and no doubt others. In Ottoman usage, the same term, usually in the plural form *re'āyā*, came to denote the general mass of the tax-paying population, as opposed to the governmental, military and religious establishments. In principle, this included both townsfolk and peasants, both Muslims and non-Muslims, but from the late eighteenth century and more especially during the nineteenth century, its application was in effect limited to non-Muslim, principally to Christian subjects of the Empire. The word reached English in two variant forms – *rayah*, from Western travellers in the Ottoman lands, and *ryot* from Muslim-ruled India, where it became the general term for a peasant.

The processes of Westernization in Middle Eastern lands added some new terms. The Ottoman (and also Persian) administrative term *tabi*, subordinate or dependent, acquired the meaning of 'subject', whence *tabiiyet*, the state of being a subject, or in other words what in modern English usage would be called nationality or citizenship. This is expressed in modern Arabic by a different term, *jinsiyya*, an abstract noun derived from *jins*. This word, possibly related to the Latin *gens*, was already in use in classical Arabic, and in various contexts could indicate type, species, class, race, nation, sex, or – in the original grammatical sense of the word – gender. The word citizen, (Latin *cives*, Greek *polites*), deriving from the Greco-Roman notion of the city and its participant members, embodies an entirely different political, and therefore semantic, tradition for which there is not even an approximately equivalent terminology. It is however surely significant that the term used to replace citizen – compatriot, or fellow-countryman – relates to another concept of identity and allegiance, expressed in such terms as country, patriot and patriotism. This too, in its political sense, is of alien origin and has undergone many transformations in the Middle East.

In the Middle East even more than elsewhere, group identity is often focused around shared memories of a common past; around events, seen as crucial, in recorded, remembered, or sometimes, imagined history.

For two of the nations of the region, the Turks and the Iranians, their identity in itself constitutes that memory, and no specific focus is needed. Their sense of group solidarity rests on the solid base of country; it is sustained by a common sense of nationhood, and upheld by centuries of sovereign independent statehood. The Turks and Persians have many memories of their national pasts, some remembered with bitterness, some with pride. The most recent of these proud memories are surely the revolutions in both countries which established the secular republic in Turkey and the Islamic republic in Iran. All these have their effect on how Turks and Persians see their own identity at home and abroad.

Among the other nations of the region, where, until modern times, the material supports and political attributes of nationhood were often lacking, the historic memory acquires even greater importance in defining identity. For Israelis, as also for many other Jews, two events define their modern identity. The first was the planned and almost completed extermination of the Jews of continental Europe, which since the 1960s has come to be known as the Holocaust. The second, in many ways a direct consequence of the first, was the establishment in 1948 of the State of Israel, seen in the Jewish perspective as a return to Zion and a rebuilding of the ancient Jewish nation in its original homeland. For the religious, it was a fulfilment of the prophecy that 'a remnant of them shall return' (Isaiah 10:20–22).

For the Palestinians and more generally the Arabs, this was not a fulfilment but a usurpation. The birth of Israel, and the failure to prevent or terminate that birth, with the consequent suffering for the Palestinians and humiliation for other Arabs, was a determining moment in modern Arab history, and the starting point of a whole series of social, cultural, and ultimately political changes. It has come to be known among Arabs as the *nakba*, or calamity. The term is an echo of the earlier *nahda*, revival or renaissance, used to denote the reawakening of Arab self-awareness and creativity after long centuries of sleep and inaction under alien rule.

Sometimes it is neither an event nor a place that sustains national self-awareness, but the memory of an individual, whose achievements are a source of pride to all those who can claim a shared identity with him. An example is the great medieval leader of the counter-Crusade, a famous hero of so many stories and legends – the mighty Saladin, who defeated the Crusaders led by Richard Lionheart of England, and recovered Jerusalem from the Christians. Until modern times, Saladin was simply a Muslim hero, and all Muslims could take pride in his victories. In modern times, this was not enough, and attempts have been made to pin an ethnic or national label on him. He has been claimed as a Turk, as an Arab, and as an Iraqi. In a sense, all these claims have some validity. Saladin rose to command in a predominantly Turkish military institution. His career was entirely in countries of Arabic speech and culture, and his historians and panegyrists wrote only in Arabic. He was born in Takrīt, the birthplace of Saddam Hussein in Iraq, and he grew to manhood in what is now Syria. From there he moved to Egypt. But if an ethnic identity must be ascribed to him, it is none of these. From the accounts of his family background preserved by the historians, it is clear that Saladin was a Kurd, and a member of a Kurdish family. This fact, previously a minor detail, has acquired new significance in our time.

For some time past it has been our practice in the Western world to proceed on the assumption that the basic determinant of both identity and loyalty, for political purposes, is that which we variously call nation or country. In American, though not in European, usage these terms are almost synonymous. In most European languages including English they are somewhat different, although there are areas of overlap. Like most of mankind, we all tend to assume that our local customs are the laws of nature. They are not. The practice of classifying people into nations and countries and of making this the primary basis of corporate political identity was until very recently local to Western Europe and to the regions colonized and settled by West Europeans. In our own time, this way of looking at people has, as a result of various circumstances, been imposed upon or adopted by most of the rest of the world. In many countries, among them countries in the Middle East, these notions are still fairly new; they are imperfectly acclimatized and even at the present time are by no means generally accepted, at least not in the sense in which they are understood and put into effect in their countries of origin.

There have, of course, always been both nations and countries in the Middle East, as elsewhere. There were countries, that is to say places; there were nations, that is to say people. Nations and sometimes also countries had names and were a familiar part of everyday life. But neither nation nor country was seen as a primary or even as a significant element in determining political identity and in directing political loyalty. In the Middle East, traditionally, these were determined on quite a different basis. Identity was expressed in and determined by religion, which in effect meant community; loyalty was owed to the state, which in practice meant the ruler and the governing elite.

During the centuries-long confrontation between the states of Europe and the Ottoman Empire, the Europeans always saw and discussed their relations in terms of Austrians, Frenchmen, Germans, Englishmen, and other nationalities versus Turks; the Turks saw it in terms of Muslims versus Christians. In pre-modern Muslim writings, the parochial subdivisions of Christendom are given scant importance. In the world-view of Muslims, which they naturally also ascribed to others, religion was the determinant of identity, the focus of loyalty and, not less important, the source of authority.

In the nineteenth century, two new concepts were introduced from Europe. One defined identity and loyalty by country – patriotism; the other by language and presumed ethnic origin – nationalism. In the Middle East, unlike Western Europe but much like Central Europe, patriotic and nationalist definitions did not coincide and often clashed. Both were alien, but both had enormous impact. The second approximated more closely to Middle Eastern realities, and had a correspondingly greater appeal.

The first of these ideas to reach the Middle East was patriotism. The place of origin was Western Europe; the point of arrival was the Ottoman Empire, a dynastic state whose multinational, multi-denominational population made it somewhat unreceptive to French or English-style patriotic appeals. It was not until after the First World War, when a relatively homogeneous Turkish nation-state emerged from the ruins of the Ottoman Empire, that patriotism took firm root. Patriotic ideas also began to affect Egypt and some other countries, but in the late nineteenth and early twentieth centuries, nationalist ideologies, of Central and East European origin, evoked a far more powerful response among the mixed populations of the old and new Empires.

The unification of Italy and still more of Germany brought hope and inspiration to many in the Middle East, who saw in these events a way to escape from the division and subjugation from which they suffered. The first state to aspire to the role of a Prussia or Sardinia was the Ottoman Empire. The Ottomans saw this role in Islamic terms – as the solidarity, perhaps eventually the unification, of the world of Islam under the leadership of the Ottoman Sultan-Caliph. Others, more open to European ideas, saw the role in ethnic terms – as the liberation and unification of various peoples, however defined, with whom they shared a common national identity.

These new political loyalties, based on patriotism and nationalism, had a special appeal for Arab Christians, more open to influences emanating from Christendom, and naturally attracted by a definition of identity which, in principle at least, would make them full and equal participants in the polity – something they could never hope to attain in a religiously defined society. The same foreign ideas – and their implications – were sometimes opposed by those who saw them as contrary to authentic Islamic values.

The attempt to return to an Islamic or, as Westerners sometimes call it, a pan-Islamic political identity, was not new. It has in the past century been encouraged by a number of Muslim rulers, including the Ottomans under both the old and the Young Turks, and the Kings of Egypt and Arabia. These state-directed campaigns of pan-Islam all failed, no doubt because they were seen, with some justification, as attempts to mobilize Islamic feelings for the purposes of one or another Muslim ruler. There was also a more popular and more radical pan-Islam, which won rather greater support. But this too was often sponsored by more radical states, and seen as serving state purposes.

When nationalist ideas of the European type first appeared in the Islamic Middle East, there were some who denounced them as divisive and irreligious. Today, after a long period during which nationalist ideologies reigned unchallenged, the same criticism is being heard again. A book by 'Abd al-Fattāh Mazlūm, entitled *The Sedition of Nationalism in the Islamic World*, argues that nationalism is the same as racism, and was introduced to the Islamic world by 'arrogant infidels', mainly Jewish, so as to divide the Muslims and turn them against one another.

But even those who oppose and reject nationalism seem unable to escape from its grip. The Turkish poet Mehmet Akif, a deeply religious man and a bitter critic of ethnic nationalism, went into self-imposed exile when the Turkish Republic was proclaimed, but one of his poems was set to music and adopted as the Turkish national anthem.

In time, these patriotic and nationalistic movements provided a new ideological expression for what was previously conceived and presented as a struggle for Islam against the infidels. The peoples of the Islamic world were acquiring new pasts, and with these new pasts came a new and different sense of their own present identity and future aspirations.

TWO

Religion

In the Middle East as elsewhere, the ancient gods were mostly local or tribal, their adherents defined by place or descent. Sometimes polytheism developed into henotheism, the belief in one supreme God who is the lord of all creation – including all the other gods. Such were the beliefs of the pre-Islamic Arabs and of some other ancient Middle Eastern peoples. In Iran, these evolved into a kind of monotheistic dualism – a belief in two supreme but unequal entities, one of good, the other of evil, engaged in a cosmic conflict, in which humanity may play an important, perhaps even a decisive role. The influence of these ideas can be seen in the later books of the Old Testament, as well as in Christianity and Islam.

In time, all these cults were replaced by the three great monotheistic religions of the Middle East – in historical sequence, Judaism, Christianity, and Islam. The older faiths were superseded, but by no means effaced. Old beliefs and habits often survived in a new guise – for example, in the veneration of holy places, holy men and even holy families. From time to time the scowl and scream of some blood-thirsty primitive cult usurp the name and worship of the universal and merciful God venerated by Jews, Christians and Muslims alike. The common Muslim blessing is 'In the name of God, the Merciful and the Compassionate'. Jews and Christians use the same or similar terms for the divine attributes. But the war-god of the terrorists knows neither mercy nor compassion, and projects an image that is both cruel and vindictive. He is also weak, needing to hire human hitmen to find and kill his enemies, and paying them with promises of carnal delights in paradise.

In the modern world, the political role of Islam, internationally as well as domestically, differs significantly from that of its peer and rival, Christianity. The heads of state or ministers of foreign affairs of the Scandinavian countries and Germany do not from time to time foregather in a Lutheran summit conference. Nor was it customary, when the Soviet Union still existed, for its rulers to join with those of Greece and Yugoslavia and, temporarily forgetting their political and ideological differences, to hold regular meetings on the basis of their current or previous adherence to the Orthodox church. Similarly, the Buddhist nations of East and Southeast Asia, the Catholic nations of southern Europe and South America, do not constitute Buddhist or Catholic blocs at the United Nations, nor for that matter in any other of their political activities.

The very idea of such a grouping, based on religious identity, might seem to many modern Western observers absurd or even comic. But it is neither absurd nor comic in relation to Islam. Some fifty-five Muslim governments, including monarchies and republics, conservatives and revolutionaries, practitioners of capitalism and disciples of various kinds of socialism, friends and enemies of the United States and exponents of a whole spectrum of shades of neutrality, have built up an elaborate apparatus of international consultation and even, on some issues, of cooperation. They hold regular high-level conferences, and, despite differences of structure, ideology, and policy, have achieved a significant measure of agreement and common action.

If we turn from international to internal politics, the difference between the Islamic countries and the rest of the world, though less dramatic, is still substantial. True, there are countries in Asia and in Europe with political parties that call themselves Buddhist or Christian. These however are few, and religious themes in the strict sense play little or no part in their appeals to the electorate. In most Islamic countries, in contrast, religion is even more powerful in internal than in international affairs.

Why this difference? Some might give the simple and obvious answer that Muslim countries are still profoundly Muslim in a way that most Christian countries are no longer Christian. Such an answer, though not lacking force, would not in itself be adequate. Christian beliefs and the Christian clergy who uphold them are still a powerful force in many Christian countries, and although their role is no longer what it was in past centuries, it is by no means insignificant. But in no Christian country at the present time can religious leaders command the degree of religious belief and the extent of religious participation by their followers that are usual in Muslim lands. More to the point, they do not exercise or even claim the kind of political role that in Muslim lands is not only common but is widely accepted as proper.

The higher level of religious faith and practice in Muslim lands as compared with those of other religions is no doubt an element in the situation, but is not in itself a sufficient explanation. The difference must rather be traced back to the very beginnings of these various religions, and to an intimate and essential relationship in Islam between religion and politics that has no parallel in any other major religion.

A basic, distinguishing feature of Islam is the all-embracing character of religion in the perception of Muslims. The Prophet, unlike earlier founders of religions, founded and governed a polity. As ruler, he promulgated laws, dispensed justice, commanded armies, made war, made peace, collected taxes, and did all the other things that a ruler does. This is reflected in the Qur'ān itself, in the biography of the Prophet, and in the traditions concerning his life and work. This distinctive quality of Islam is most vividly illustrated in the injunction which occurs not once but several times in the Qur'ān (3:104, 110; 7:157; 22:41, etc.), by which Muslims are instructed as to their basic duty, which is 'to command good and forbid evil' – not just to do good and avoid evil, a personal duty imposed by all religions, but to command good and forbid evil, that is to say, to exercise authority to that end. Under the Prophet's immediate successors, in the formative period of Islamic doctrine and law, his state became an empire in which Muslims conquered and subjugated non-Muslims. This meant that in Islam there was from the beginning an interpenetration of religion and government, of belief and power, which has some parallel in Old Testament Judaism but not in any subsequent form.

Christian theory and practice evolved along other lines. The founder of Christianity is quoted as saying, 'Render unto to Caesar the things which are Caesar's and unto God the things which are God's.' In this familiar and much-quoted dictum, a principle is laid down, at the very beginning of Christianity, that remained fundamental to Christian thought and practice and is discernible throughout Christian history. Always there were two authorities, God and Caesar, dealing with different matters, exercising different jurisdictions; each with its own laws and its own courts to enforce them; each with its own institutions and its own hierarchy to administer them.

These two different authorities are what, in the Western world, we call Church and State. In Christendom they have always both been there, sometimes in association, sometimes in conflict; sometimes one predominating, sometimes the other – but always two and not one. In Muslim theory, Church and State are not separate or separable institutions. The mosque is a building, a place of worship and of study.

The same is true of the synagogue. Neither term was used by its own worshippers to denote an ecclesiastical institution comparable with the church in Christendom. Classical Islamic thought and practice distinguish between the things of this world and the things of the other, and the different groups of people who look after them, but the same Holy Law regulates both. Such familiar pairs of words as lay and ecclesiastical, sacred and profane, spiritual and temporal, and the like, have no equivalents in classical Arabic or in other Islamic languages, since the dichotomy which they express, deeply rooted in Christendom, was unknown in Islam until comparatively modern times. Its introduction was the result of external influences, and its vocabulary consists of borrowed words, made-up words, or old words injected with new meanings. In recent years those external influences have been attacked and weakened, and the ideas which they brought, never accepted by more than a relatively small and alienated elite, have also begun to weaken. And as external influences lose their appeal, there is an inevitable return to older, more deep-rooted perceptions.

There are some further differences. Christianity arose amid the fall of an empire. The rise of Christianity parallels the decline of Rome, and the Church created its own structures to survive in this period. During the centuries when Christianity was a persecuted faith of the downtrodden, God was seen as subjecting His followers to suffering and tribulation to test and purify their faith. When Christianity finally became a state religion, Christians tried to take over and refashion the institutions and even the language of Rome to serve their own needs.

Islam in contrast rose amid the birth of an empire, and became the creed of a vast, triumphant and flourishing realm, created under the aegis of the new faith and expressed in the language – Arabic – of the new revelation. While for Saint Augustine and other early Christian thinkers the State was a lesser evil, for Muslims the State – that is of course the Islamic state – was a divine good, ordained by holy law to promulgate God's faith, enforce God's law and protect and increase God's people. In this perception of the universe, God is seen as helping rather than testing the believers, as desiring their success in this world, and as manifesting His divine approval by victory and dominance, for His army, His community, and His state. Martyrdom, in the Muslim definition, means death in battle in a holy war for the faith. A partial exception to this triumphalism is constituted by the Shī'a, the defeated faction in the early struggles for the caliphate. Defeat and repression gave the Shī'a an almost Christian-style conception of suffering, passion and martyrdom. In modern times this has combined with new ideologies and new technologies to produce an explosively powerful social force.

These perceptions from the remoter Islamic past still have important consequences for the present time, notably in their effect on the shaping of Muslim self-awareness. For most of the recorded history of most of the Muslim world, the primary and basic definition of identity, both adoptive and ascriptive, is religion. And for Muslims, that of course means Islam or, more specifically, the particular version of Islam to which they adhere. Whatever other factors may have been at work, in order to become effective they had to assume a religious or at least a sectarian form. In the modern secular West and other regions that have accepted Western ways, the world is divided into nations, and the nation may be subdivided into different religious communities. In the Muslim perception, the world is divided into religions, and these may be subdivided into nations and, by abuse, states.

This basic religious identity still persists in popular sentiment, and has recently been extended even to the domain of nuclear weaponry. The argument has sometimes been heard that since the West, for this purpose including Russia, possesses Christian bombs, and Israel is reputed to have a Jewish bomb, it is only fitting and indeed necessary that one or more Muslim countries should acquire or produce an Islamic bomb. This point was often made in the wave of exultation that passed through many Muslim countries when Pakistan successfully detonated six nuclear devices in May 1998. An explicit disclaimer by the Prime Minister of Pakistan, during a visit to Saudi Arabia, of any religious identity for his bomb did little to discourage this response.

Where Islam is perceived as the main basis of identity, it necessarily constitutes the main claim to allegiance. In most Muslim countries the essential distinction between loyalty and disloyalty is indeed provided by religion. The prime test in Islam, unlike Christianity, is not adherence to correct belief and doctrine, though these are not unimportant; what matters most is communal loyalty and conformity. And since religious conformity is the outward sign of loyalty, it follows that heresy is disloyalty and apostasy is treason. Classical Islam had no hierarchic institution to define and impose correct belief, to detect and punish incorrect belief. The Muslims, instead, laid great stress on consensus, both as a source of guidance and as a basis for legitimacy. Despite the vast changes of the last two centuries, Islam itself has clearly remained the most widely accepted form of consensus in Muslim countries, far more potent than political programs or slogans; Islamic symbols and appeals are still the most effective for social mobilization.

It is useful to remember that the word 'Islam' is commonly used in two different senses – as the counterpart of 'Christianity', that is to say the name of a religion, a system of belief and worship, and also as the counterpart of 'Christendom', denoting a whole civilization which developed under the aegis of that religion. There has been much confusion among outside observers who, failing to recognize this distinction, have often attributed to the Islamic religion certain widespread doctrines and practices which, though important in the Muslim past or present, are as remote from original Islam as are Crusaders and Inquisitors from original Christianity. Muslim militants and radicals have always been keenly aware of these differences, and have invoked what they perceive as authentic, pristine Islam against the innovations and falsifications of those who pretend to rule in its name. They have also introduced some innovations of their own.

In principle, Islam has neither priests nor church. The imams are merely leaders in prayer; the ulema, scholars in theology and jurisprudence, but with no priestly office; the mosque simply a place. In the early phases of Islamic history, this was indeed so, but with the passage of time, imams and ulema acquired professional training and certification, and became, in the sociological if not in the theological sense, a clergy, albeit without sacraments. The mosque remained only a building, but the ulema grouped themselves in hierarchies, with higher and lower ranks. The interpretation and administration of the holy law, for which they were primarily responsible, gave them power, status, influence, and sometimes also wealth. These developments were no doubt assisted by the example of the Christian churches in the countries which the Muslims conquered, notably the former Byzantine territories incorporated in the Ottoman Empire. The, so to speak, Christianization of Islamic ecclesiastical institutions has reached its apogee in the present-day Islamic Republic of Iran where, for the first time in Muslim history, we find the functional equivalents of bishops, archbishops, cardinals, and – some would argue – even a pope. These Christian influences are of course purely organizational and brought no corresponding acceptance of Christian doctrines or values. But the rulers of Iran have indeed created an Islamic church, claiming both spiritual and temporal authority. They may soon confront an Islamic reformation.

Islamic identity is not monolithic. In Egypt and generally in Muslim North Africa, Islam is overwhelmingly Sunni and, since Shī'ism is virtually unknown, the difference is not felt to be important. Turkey too was long regarded as an exclusively Sunni country, but in recent years, thanks to the growth of democratic institutions, the previously silent Shī'ite minorities have become increasingly visible and vocal. In Iran, alone among the Muslim countries of the

Middle East and North Africa, Shī'a Islam is the dominant and official faith, and some have seen in the Persian espousal of Shī'ism a way of asserting their distinctive Persian identity against their predominantly Sunni Arab, Turkish, Central Asian and Indian neighbours. But there are sizable Sunni minorities in Iran, notably in the eastern provinces, among Turkic and Baluchi speakers.

Arab Southwest Asia shows significant differences. Palestinians and Jordanians are Sunni, but elsewhere, in Syria, Lebanon, Iraq and nowadays even in the eastern provinces of Saudi Arabia and some of the Gulf sheikhdoms, there are substantial Shī'a populations. In Lebanon they are now the largest single group and are increasingly demanding a corresponding change in their place in the Lebanese polity. In Iraq as a whole, and even in its capital, Baghdad, they by now constitute a majority of the population. They have always been subject to a Sunni ascendancy that has continued without significant change from Turkish through British times to the independent monarchy and the present day 'republic'.

As well as the mainstream, the so-called 'Twelver' Shī'a – the established faith in Iran – there are deviant groups within the Shī'a camp. Notable among these are the Alawis, previously known as Nusayrīs, in Syria, where they form approximately twelve per cent of the population. That twelve per cent however, includes the President and much of the ruling establishment. The same name, Alawis, has long been applied to a variety of non-Sunni Muslims in Turkey, professing different forms of Shī'ite beliefs and Sufi mystical practices.

There are other smaller groups deviating from what one might call the mainstream Shī'a. One of these is the Ismā'īlī sect with two branches, claiming some thousands of followers in central Syria, and much larger numbers in India, Pakistan, Central Asia and East Africa. Of greater importance in the region are the Druze, an offshoot of the Ismā'īlīs, with followers in Syria, Lebanon, Jordan and

Israel. In the last named country, they are the only part of the Arab population which, at the request of their own leaders, performs military service.

In every country of the Middle East except Israel, and until recently, Lebanon, Islam is the religion of the majority. It was not always so. At the time of the advent of Islam and the Arab conquests in the seventh century, most of the inhabitants of Iran followed one or another form of the Zoroastrian faith. West of Iran, the majority of the inhabitants were Christians, not only in the provinces subject to the Christian Empire of Byzantium, but even in Aramaic-speaking Iraq, then part of the Persian Empire. These Christians were of various churches, some of them, notably in Egypt and Syria, in schism with the Orthodox Church of Constantinople.

The only other surviving religion of any significance was Judaism, represented by communities in all these countries, including, at that time, Arabia. The major centres of Jewish life and thought were in Iraq, under Persian rule, and in the former Jewish homeland, which its Roman and Byzantine rulers called Palestine.

Most of the first converts to Islam were pagan Arabians. Later converts were recruited from the Zoroastrian, Christian and Jewish communities of southwest Asia, North Africa, and, for a while, southern Europe. In the course of time, Islam came to be the majority religion. But the others remained, and most of the countries of the region have, or until recently had, religious minorities of one kind or another. The Zoroastrians have shrunk to some tens of thousands in Iran, with a somewhat larger number descended from Persian *émigrés* who fled to the Indian subcontinent. They are still known there as Parsees, after their country of origin. Christians and Jews remain in much larger numbers.

In Saudi Arabia, in accordance with a ruling dating back to the seventh-century caliph Umar, no other religion is permitted, and non-Muslims (Christians but not Jews) are admitted only as temporary visitors, and confined to certain designated areas. No non-Muslim is allowed to set foot in the holy cities of Mecca and Medina in the Hejaz. In other parts of the Arabian Peninsula and the adjoining islands, small Jewish minorities survived until fairly recently; Christians disappeared at an early date. In Egypt and the Fertile Crescent, both Christians and Jews lived under Muslim rule until the present time. Some Christians remain; the Jews have all but disappeared. In North Africa, perhaps because of its nearness to the European Christian enemy, Christianity died out at an early date. Jewish minorities survived much longer, and were even reinforced in the fifteenth and sixteenth centuries by the arrival of Jewish refugees from Christian Europe.

The oldest and most creative of the Arab Jewish communities – the most fully identified with the country and people of which they were a part – were the Jews of Iraq. Jews had lived in Iraq since the days of the Babylonian captivity and are – or rather were – profoundly rooted in the soil. Compared with them, the Arabs of Iraq are newcomers, dating only from the seventh century CE. The Jews of Iraq adopted Arabic at an early date, and except for some minor particularities, shared the language, culture and way of life of their Muslim compatriots. After the establishment of the separate state of Iraq in 1920, they were of course Iraqis. In the heyday of European-style patriotism they too, like their Christian compatriots, saw themselves and in some nationalist circles were seen as Arabs. In the 1920s and 30s some Iraqi Jews joined with other Iraqis in rejecting what they described as the alien implantation of European Jews in Arab Palestine.

This dream of Iraqi brotherhood was gradually weakened by the struggle for Palestine and still more by the extremely effective propaganda of Nazi Germany. The dream was violently ended in June 1941, when the first major attack on a modern Jewish community in an Arab land took place in Baghdad, in the brief interval between the collapse of the pro-Axis Rashid Ali regime and the arrival of the royalist and British troops. This was followed by numerous other outbreaks of anti-Jewish violence in Iraq, Syria, Egypt, Southern Arabia, and North Africa, in which hundreds were killed or injured and many more rendered destitute by the destruction of their homes and workplaces.

These attacks and the resulting flight of Jews pre-dated the establishment of the state of Israel, and no doubt contributed to its creation. That event, and the ensuing war, further undermined their position, and led to the flight of the remaining Jewish communities – sometimes, as in Iraq and Yemen, with the cooperation of the governments of those countries – and their transfer to Israel. At the present time the only Arab country with a significant Jewish community is Morocco, and that too is being reduced by voluntary emigration. The long and distinguished history of the Jews in Arab lands appears to be drawing to an end. Small Jewish communities remain in Turkey and Iran. In the former, their official status is that of equal citizens in a secular state; in the latter, of tolerated and protected subjects of an Islamic state. Their numbers, in both countries, have in recent years been greatly reduced by emigration, much of it to Israel.

The decline of the Christian communities was, except in Lebanon, less traumatic. But the overall trend, both demographic and political, has been unmistakably against them. In Lebanon, they emerged from the long and bitter civil wars with depleted numbers and reduced power. In Turkey and Iran, both Christian and Jewish minorities survive, but play no significant part in public life. Except for the old-established Persian-speaking Jews, these minorities, unlike those in the Arab countries, were until recently linguistically and culturally as well as religiously different from the Muslim majorities.

The Christians, though much fewer in numbers than the Muslims, exhibit far greater sectarian variety. There are some Protestants, resulting from the activities of European and American missionaries from the nineteenth century onwards, and much larger numbers of Catholics, most of them Uniates, from various eastern churches that at one

time or another entered into communion with Rome. And
then there are of course the Eastern Churches, offering a
wide spectrum of the theological and ecclesiastical history of
Christendom in the first thousand years of the Christian era.
Followers of the Orthodox Church, irrespective of their
ethnic affiliations, are still known as *Rūm*.

Among Jews there are no comparable sectarian differences, but there are major cultural differences. The most
important of these is the distinction between the indigenous
Middle Eastern Jews, historically and culturally part of the
world of Islam, and the European Jews, culturally and
historically part of Christendom. The many contrasts
and occasional clashes between these two groups in Israel
reflect, in miniature, the larger confrontation of Christendom and Islam. These encounters affect, and are affected
by, the looming conflict between the religious and secular
interpretations of Israeli and, ultimately, of Jewish
identity.

The Jews who settled in Israel came, overwhelmingly,
from countries of two civilizations, from Christendom and
the lands of Islam. Inevitably, they brought with them much
of the civilization of the countries from which they came,
including their perceptions and definitions of identity. Any
one who has visited Israel will recognize the difference
between, for example, Jews from Berlin and Jews from
Baghdad, not in their Jewishness, but in the German culture
of the one, and the Iraqi Arab culture of the other. But this
contrast goes beyond city or country; it arises from the
difference between the two civilizations, Christian and
Muslim, that meet in this small Jewish state and community.
The much discussed distinction between Ashkenazic and
Sefardic Jews, in purely Jewish terms, is only about minor
differences of ritual, each recognizing the other as valid.
This distinction has no theological or legal significance. Nor
does the difference, as some explain it in currently fashionable terms, arise from the conflict between Euro-American
and Afro-Asian Jews. The really profound dividing line is
between what one might call the 'Christian' Jews and the

'Muslim' Jews, using these terms with a civilizational, not a religious connotation. The Jewish immigrants to Israel brought with them, from their countries of origin, much of their cultures of origin, and it was therefore inevitable that there should have been disagreements and even clashes between them.

The State of Israel thus brings together, with a common citizenship and a common religion, representatives of two major religiously-defined civilizations, in both of which they had played a minor but significant role. The Jews had of course their own religious culture, which remained authentically Jewish, though profoundly influenced by the dominant religious cultures of the countries from which they came. But since the destruction of the ancient Jewish state, there has been no real Jewish political culture. Jews as individuals may have at times participated, in a subordinate capacity, in the political process. Jewish communal leaders did at times have some powers over their own people, but they were always limited powers under delegated authority – greater under Muslim rule, smaller under Christian rule, but always delegated, limited, and revocable. There was no Jewish sovereign power. The memories of ancient Jewish sovereignty were too remote, the experience of modern Jewish sovereignty too brief, to provide much in the way of guidance. There is of course extensive discussion of the state and its business in Jewish religious literature, but since the participants, for the most part, had no access to the power of the state, their arguments are overwhelmingly abstract and theoretical – or, to put it in different terms, messianic. In the absence of an explicitly Jewish political culture based on experience, it is in politics, more than anything else, that the culture of Israel is derivative. The countries of origin offer a variety of examples: clergyman and ulema, bishops and muftis, archbishops and ayatollahs or, looking perhaps in a different direction, crusade and jihad, inquisitors and assassins. The recent immigrants from the countries of the former Soviet Union brought some additional models – commissars and apparatchiks and other elements of Soviet political society, including the use of the party as a kind of an established church.

These groups bring with them very different cultural traditions on such matters as the relations between politics and religion, between power and wealth, and more generally, on the manner in which power is attained, exercised, and transferred. In Israel there have of late been increasing signs of Middle Eastern attitudes on these matters. If this trend continues, Israel will develop greater affinities with the region in which it is situated. This will not necessarily make for better relations. It could indeed have the opposite effect, and might even endanger the qualitative edge which has enabled Israel to flourish in a predominantly hostile environment.

In Muslim countries, the rapid transformation of society, culture, and above all the state presents the leaders of organized religion with new problems, for which their own history offers no precedent, their traditional literature no explicit guidance. The establishment of a Jewish state has also confronted Jews, for the first time since antiquity, with the problem of the relationship between religion and government – in Muslim terms, between the affairs of this world and the next; in Christian terms, between church and state, between God and Caesar. Christians did indeed find a solution for the resulting dilemma. It took centuries of bitter religious war and persecution before they arrived at that solution. But most Christian countries have by now accepted it, in practice if not always in law. It is the solution known as the separation of church and state. This device achieves a double purpose. On the one hand it prevents the state from interfering in affairs of religion; on the other, it prevents the exponents of one or other brand of religion from using the power of the state to enforce their doctrines or their rules.

For a long time the encounter between church and state was seen as a purely Christian problem, not relevant to Jews or Muslims, and separation as a Christian solution to a

Christian dilemma. Looking at the contemporary Middle East, both Muslim and Jewish, one must ask whether this is still true; or whether Muslims and Jews, having perhaps caught a Christian disease, might consider a Christian remedy.

Race and Language

The first, primal and indelible mark of identity is race. In some parts of the world this is still of overriding importance. Except perhaps in Arabia, where slavery was not abolished until 1962, in the Middle East race matters less. In most of the region, amid the many differences of language, religion, culture, nationality and country, the racial mix shows only minor variations, and these evoke only minor concern – social snobbery rather than social discrimination. It is true that in the course of the centuries vast numbers of aliens came into the region, occasionally as conquerors, continuously as slaves. But neither group left any noticeable remnant. The common use of female slaves as concubines, the castration of males to meet the consequent need for eunuchs to guard them, combined to prevent the formation in the Middle East of recognizable, racially alien populations of slaves, ex-slaves and their descendants, such as are found in the Americas. Except on the fringes of the region, as in the Sudan and Mauritania, there are no significant numbers of blacks. White newcomers – both slaves and conquerors – were similarly assimilated into the Middle Eastern mix.

For a long time now identity in the Middle East has been overwhelmingly male. Rank, status, kinship, ethnic and even religious identity are determined by the male line. In Islamic law, intermarriage with other monotheistic religions is allowed, but only between a Muslim male and a non-Muslim female, who is even permitted to retain her religion. Marriage between a non-Muslim male and a Muslim woman, on the other hand, is a capital offence. The doctors of the Holy law explain their reasoning: in any encounter between Islam and another creed, Islam must dominate, and in a marriage it is the male that dominates. In the royal houses of Europe, genealogists set forth in loving detail the precise descent of kings and princes, on both the male and distaff sides. Among the sultans and shahs of Islam, in most times and places, only the names of the fathers were normally known. The mothers, more often than not, were nameless slave concubines in the harem, and their names, personalities and origins, with rare exceptions, were of no concern, and indeed of no interest to historians and others.

It was not always so. In antiquity there were females among the gods and heroes; there were princesses and even reigning queens on earth. The names of Semiramis of Assyria, Nefertiti of Egypt and Zenobia of Arabia are still remembered. The Bible tells of the matriarchs as well as of the patriarchs and portrays some remarkable females – Deborah, Ruth and Esther among the good ones, Jezebel among the bad. In ancient Arabia, mothers as well as fathers figured in the proud lists of ancestors; in the Umayyad caliphate, only the sons of known, free, and noble Arab mothers could be considered for the succession. Those who were born to non-Arab and slave mothers were systemically excluded. Among the Jews, rabbinic law defined a Jew as one who was born to a Jewish mother or converted to Judaism. The child of a Jewish mother and a non-Jewish father was born a Jew; the child of a Jewish father and a non-Jewish mother was not. This ruling gave a defining role to the Jewish mother, even though its origins may lie in the principle expressed by the Roman jurists with their usual lapidary brevity: 'Mater certa, pater incertus' (mother certain, father uncertain). Muslims, preferring patrilineal rather than matrilineal identity, tried to achieve the same certitude by an increasingly elaborate apparatus of seclusion and protection surrounding their women.

The major change dates from the mid-eighth century, with the so-called Abbasid revolution – the replacement of the Umayyad by the Abbasid caliphate. As so often with revolutions, the process of change both preceded and followed the transfer of power. The last of the Umayyad caliphs was the son of a slave woman; the first of the Abbasid caliphs was the son of a free Arab lady. But among his successors, and in almost all the subsequent dynasties of sultans and shahs, the harem became the norm, and the mothers of the sultans were usually slave concubines. Since Muslim law categorically prohibits the enslavement of free Muslims or even of free non-Muslim subjects of the Muslim state, this meant that the concubines were in principle of alien origin. In the Ottoman line, they included elements as diverse as Circassians and other Caucasians, Slavs and other East Europeans, and even occasional Westerners, supplied by the Barbary Corsairs.

To a somewhat lesser extent, a similar process may be observed among rich and powerful Muslim families. Richer men tended to have Circassian and other white concubines, while less affluent slaveowners made do with lower-priced Ethiopians and Nubians. Even this, though it led in places to some economic shading of complexion, did not create serious social problems or even politically significant racial consciousness. Polygamy, and more especially concubinage, served to prevent the emergence of well-defined racial groups and of a strong sense of racial identity. For the racist, fathers and mothers are equally important in defining identity, and in a racially tense situation persons of mixed parentage are regarded with suspicion by both sides. In a society where conquerors lawfully and normally enslaved the conquered and where male owners enjoyed sexual rights over their female slaves, a significant population of mixed parentage soon emerged. If, as eventually happened in most of the Middle East, these are deemed to inherit the status of their fathers, then, before long, racial distinctions become blurred.

In the early years after the great Arab conquests of the seventh century, a social and even political distinction was maintained between Arab Muslims and non-Arab converts to Islam, and, to a lesser extent, between full Arabs and half-Arabs, that is, the sons of an Arab father and a foreign mother (the reverse was not envisaged). In the second century of the Muslim era such distinctions were abandoned and – except perhaps as a kind of aristocratic pride of lineage – forgotten.

This has not prevented the increasing use of 'racist' as a term of abuse in Middle Eastern polemics. Except among fundamentalists, and to some extent even among them, the modern language of politics, particularly of political abuse, has become largely Western. Even the most anti-Western seem to prefer fashionable European terms; 'nazi' and 'racist' are now the most popular ways to insult and condemn an opponent. Neither of these terms has much relevance to Middle Eastern realities. The one exception is anti-Semitism, which has spread widely all over the Arab world, and beyond to other Islamic countries. This exception however is more apparent than real. Arab anti-Semitism is not racist in the European sense, though it often uses racist images, stereotypes, and language, all of them borrowed or adapted from Europe. This hostility is primarily religious, secondarily national, and is increasingly being expressed in Islamic rather than European terms. It is, however, noteworthy that in current political polemics in the Middle East, some prominent Christians of Jewish or part-Jewish background are routinely referred to as Jews.

According to a race theory widely adopted in parts of Europe in the first half of this century, humanity is divided into a number of clearly defined races, unchanging and unequal. In Europe and the Middle East, according to this theory, there were two main races, the Aryans who were superior, and the Semites who were inferior and indeed noxious. The Jews and the Arabs belonged to the inferior Semitic race; the Persians to the superior Aryan race. The status of the Turks was a matter of debate among race theorists. Clearly, they were not Semites, but there was some question as to whether they could be considered as part of the superior Aryan race, or belonged to the less distinguished Altaic stock.

This view of humanity was officially established in Nazi Germany, and enjoyed a considerable following elsewhere. It had, however, very little impact in the Middle East. Neither the Jews nor the Arabs described themselves as Semites; they had other, more accurate and more relevant ways of defining themselves and their adversaries. Even the Nazis attached very little importance to racial distinctions in their dealings with the Middle East. In addition to their putative Aryan brethren, they also made a significant effort to court Turks and Arabs. Among the latter especially, for reasons quite unrelated to race, they were able to win some response. They soon made it clear that their anti-Semitism, in both doctrine and policy, was concerned only with Jews, and with none of the other so-called Semitic peoples. An attempt was even made during the war by a committee of German Middle East experts to persuade Hitler to authorize a revised edition of *Mein Kampf*, replacing 'Semite', 'Semitic', 'anti-Semitic', wherever they occurred with 'Jew', 'Jewish', and 'anti-Jewish'. This proposal was not accepted, and the canon remained sacrosanct, but in practical application it was clear and well-understood that for German anti-Semites, Semites meant Jews. No other Semites were affected, and indeed the so-called Semitic Arabs were treated rather better by the Nazis than the so-called Aryan Czechs, Poles, and Russians. This de facto redefinition of anti-Semitism later facilitated its acceptance, under other names, in some Arab and Islamic countries.

Nazi propaganda was active in Turkey before and still more during the Second World War. It evoked a limited response, mostly confined to extremist pan-Islamic and more especially pan-Turkish groups. Both were naturally drawn to a power that seemed to promise the dismemberment of the Soviet Union, and the freeing – at least from Russian domination – of its Muslim and Turkish peoples. Some even found, in Nazi race theories, a model for their own ideology of pan-Turkism. All in all, however, the impact of racism in Turkey was limited.

The Persians were another matter. The ancient name of their country, Iran, is in origin the same word as Aryan. It was used in the titles of the ancient pre-Islamic kings of Iran, and occurs in early Arabic historical and geographical writings following the Arab conquest in the seventh century. It enjoyed a new popularity with the literary revival of the old Persian myths from the tenth century onwards, but did not come into general use as the name of the country until the late nineteenth century.

The name Persia is derived from that of the southwestern province, called Pārs in antiquity, and Fārs after the Arab conquest, since the Arabic script has no letter for P. The idiom of the province became the national language; the name of the province, in various forms, came to be the name of the whole country. But only in foreign usage. In Arabic, the Persians, but not Persia, were called *Furs*. Persians speaking in their own language called that language Fārsī, and generally referred to the different parts of their country by regional names.

In the course of the nineteenth century, Persians began, more frequently, to refer to the modern realm of the Shahs by the ancient name Iran. This practice gained force from the rediscovery, in the early twentieth century, of the ancient history of Iran, thanks largely to European archeologists and philologists.

A new element was injected in the 1930s, through the increasingly close involvement of Germany in Iranian economic development, and the consequent growth of Nazi ideological influence. In March 1935, the name of the country was officially changed, in all languages, from Persia to Iran; the following year the German economics minister, Dr Hjalmar Schacht, on a visit to Iran, assured the Iranians that since they were 'pure Aryans', the anti-Semitic Nuremberg race laws did not apply to them.

The same dubious privilege was accorded by the Third Reich to the Kurds and to the Armenians. Some of the latter responded by founding an Armenian National-Socialist organization called Hossank and by forming a number of Armenian battalions to serve with the German forces. They were recruited among Red Army prisoners of war and the Armenian diaspora in German-occupied Europe, with some volunteers from North America, who saw in this an opportunity to liberate Armenia from Soviet rule. The Nazis were able to raise similar formations, no doubt inspired by similar hopes, among other diasporas and among prisoners of war from other imperial armies. These included Turkic peoples from Central Asia, Arabs from the Middle East and North Africa, as well as a variety of 'Aryans' from Soviet Transcaucasia and British India. None of these reached significant numbers.

'Semite' and 'Aryan' belong to the same vocabulary, and have undergone the same perversions. Both date from the beginnings of modern philology in the eighteenth and nineteenth centuries, and from the momentous discovery that languages could be classified into cognate groups or families. In 1781, a German philologist called August Ludwig Schlözer suggested the term Semitic, from Noah's son Shem, to designate the family of languages to which Assyrian, Hebrew, Aramaic, Arabic and Ethiopic belong. Similarly the term Aryan, meaning 'noble' and used by the ancient inhabitants of Persia and India to describe themselves, was adopted as the name of a group of related languages including Sanskrit, Old Persian, and some others. As far back as 1861 the great German philologist Max Müller pointed out that confusing the history of languages with the history of races would falsify everything. Nevertheless, race theorists, particularly those anxious to establish their own uniqueness and superiority, eagerly seized on this new vocabulary, and misappropriated it to their own use.

The defeat of Nazi Germany in 1945, and the discovery of the appalling crimes that had been committed in the name of racism, brought a change of attitude and, consequently, of usage. But not completely. Few nowadays outside the lunatic fringes would use the word 'Aryan' as a racial designation, but the same taboo does not apply to the equally tainted and misleading use of the word 'Semite'. Even otherwise respectable writers and journals sometimes permit themselves such pronouncements as that 'the Jews and Arabs are both Semites'. If this statement has any meaning at all, it is that Hebrew and Arabic are both Semitic languages.

That is not unimportant. The fact that such basic elements of language as family terms and numbers are recognizably similar can surely influence attitudes, and confirm the sense of kinship fostered by their religious traditions. Isaac and Ishmael, according to both the Bible and the Qur'ān, were brothers, and were the ancestors respectively of the Jews and of the Arabs. The use of the term 'cousin' (in Arabic *ibn 'amm* – literally, son of uncle), by each to designate the other, expresses this sense of kinship. But insofar as it exists, it is the accepted and familiar kinship of family, not the alien notion of race. Such kinship does not necessarily make for better relations. It can indeed have the opposite effect, in a region where feuding between tribes, or even between families within tribes, has continued from remote antiquity to the present day. Nor is there any evidence that speakers of Arabic, Hebrew, Aramaic and some of the languages of Ethiopia feel any special affinity because their mother tongues belong to the family that European philologists called Semitic.

Language is indeed in many ways a primary mark of identity. Acquired in infancy, the aptly named mother-tongue brings with it a whole world of memories, associations, allusions and values. It serves as a bond of unity with others who share it, and a barrier against those who don't. For all but a few, this remains so throughout life, and no process of conversion or naturalization can obliterate the difference between the native speaker and one who has acquired the language. This difference has indeed been a matter of life and death, as in the famous story of how the Ephraimites were identified and killed because they could not pronounce the word 'Shibboleth' (Judges 12:5,6). A modern parallel was the use, during the struggles in Lebanon, of the Arabic word for tomato as a shibboleth to distinguish between Lebanese and Palestinians; the one group said 'bandūra' the other 'banadūra'. Both come from the Italian pomodoro.

Unlike some other regions of ancient civilization, the Middle East had many languages, and the resulting confusion is vividly illustrated in the Bible story of the Tower of Babel and the divine decision to 'confound their language, that they may not understand one another's speech' (Genesis 11:7). Many of these languages were local and ephemeral, but a significant number became languages of civilization, of government, religion and literature, each with its own script. Most of them have long since disappeared. Their numbers were greatly and constantly reduced by immigration and colonization, by conquest and empire, by religious change and cultural influence.

At the beginning of the Christian era there were only three areas in which indigenous languages were still in common use in both spoken and written forms; these are Persian, Coptic and Aramaic. In the East, in the Empire of Iran, a form of Persian was the sacred language of the Zoroastrian faith and the official language of the Sasanid state. The more ancient forms of Persian, written in the cuneiform and other scripts, had been abandoned, and the Persian of that time was written in a script adapted from the Aramaic alphabet.

The Christianization of Egypt produced a similar result. The old Egyptian hieroglyphic writing was forgotten, and the last form of the ancient Egyptian language, Coptic, written in a script adapted from the Greek, was the medium of Christian scripture and other literature. In the central lands of the Fertile Crescent, Aramaic, spoken in various dialects and written in various scripts, had replaced the more ancient languages. Assyrian and Babylonian, Phoenician and all the other Canaanite languages except one, had disappeared. That one was Hebrew, which alone survived because of its religious importance and above all because of the Hebrew Bible. But it was no longer spoken. By the beginning of the Christian era, the Jews, like everyone else in the Fertile Crescent, spoke Aramaic and even produced much of their religious literature, notably the Talmud, in that language. Hebrew survived mainly in scripture and prayer, and these too were often translated into Aramaic, written in the Hebrew script.

Alien languages, first Greek and then Latin, also had a major impact, and there is no lack of classical loanwords and loan translations in Middle Eastern languages, including even post-Biblical Hebrew and Qur'ānic Arabic. With the advent of Islam and the Arab coⱂquest in the seventh century, Latin and Greek disappeared, and there was no recognizable foreign linguistic influence until modern times.

Hellenization, Romanization and above all Christianization had combined to obliterate much of the ancient languages, cultures and identities of the Middle East. Islamization and Arabization completed the process, and before long the ancient languages were not spoken, the ancient scripts were not written and could no longer be read. Nor was there any motive to make the effort.

Aramaic and Coptic both survived into the Islamic era. Aramaic, in various forms, was the common language of the Christian majority, a Jewish minority and a dwindling pagan remnant. Today it is still spoken – but not written – by small village populations in a few remote areas in Syria, Iraq, Turkey and Iran, most of them Christian, or, until recently, Jewish. They are all disappearing through emigration or assimilation. Coptic continued to be spoken for a while, mainly in upper Egypt, but seems to have died out by the eighteenth century. Both Coptic and Aramaic remained in use in written form in the rituals and scriptures of the

Eastern churches. In all other respects they have been supplanted by Arabic.

Until the nineteenth century, Hebrew too was primarily a language of scripture, of religion, scholarship and literature, and in some limited measure, of communication between Jews from different countries. The revival of Hebrew in modern times was inspired by a combination of religion and nationalism; it was made possible, even necessary, by the coming together of Jews of diverse origins and many languages, and the pressing need for a common language acceptable to all of them. Yiddish-speaking Jews and Arabic-speaking Jews disdained to learn each other's idioms; but both could agree on the sacred language of scripture and of their forebears. Hebrew reborn was a powerful force in the creation of a new Israeli identity.

Within a remarkably short time of the great Arab conquests in the seventh centuries, Arabic, previously limited to the Arabian peninsula and to the desert borderlands of the Fertile Crescent, became the dominant and in time the majority language of most of the Middle East and North Africa. The Qur'ān made it the language of scripture; the Sharī'a, the language of law. The Arab empire made it the language of government and eventually of administration; the new and rich civilization that flourished under the aegis of the caliphs made it a vehicle of literature, scholarship and science. Except in Iran, it permanently replaced the older written languages of civilization and, to a remarkable extent, even the spoken languages of the cities and the countryside. Even those who retained their Christian or Jewish faith in time adopted Arabic, not only of necessity, as the language of communication and commerce, but even as the language of much of their own religious literatures.

They did however retain their own alphabets, sanctified by scripture, commentary and ritual. The Arabic script was that of the Qur'ān, and for a long time, Christians and Jews, even though they spoke and wrote Arabic, were not yet prepared to adopt the Arabic script in their own internal writings. A similar situation arose in Europe, where the

Latin alphabet was associated with the Christian state and church. European Jews spoke the same languages as their compatriots, but they preferred to write them in the Hebrew script, with a sprinkling of Hebrew words, thus creating Judaeo-French, Judaeo-Spanish, Judaeo-German, Judaeo-Italian and the rest. For the same reasons, Muslims in reconquered Spain wrote Spanish in the Arabic script, thereby preserving their Muslim identity. In the Middle East, Christians produced a considerable literature written in the Arabic language and in the Syriac script, known as Karshuni. Arabic-speaking and Persian-speaking Jews wrote Arabic and Persian in the alphabet of the Old Testament. The normal practice was to use the Arabic script when writing on science, medicine and other topics of general interest, but the Hebrew script when writing on matters of religion and religious law. In the same way, Turkish-speaking Christian communities in Anatolia, belonging to different churches, preferred to write Turkish in the Greek or Armenian script. There are surviving manuscripts in Judaeo-Turkish, that is to say in Ottoman Turkish written in the Hebrew script, and a kind of Judaeo-Turkish has survived among Turkic peoples outside the Ottoman Empire. But in the Ottoman lands it was swamped by the massive arrival of Jewish refugees from Spain in the fifteenth and sixteenth centuries, bringing with them Judaeo-Spanish, the literary form of which is known as Ladino. This remained the dominant language of the Jews of Turkey until the twentieth century, where it finally gave way to standard Turkish. Karshuni writing and Judaeo-Arabic have similarly become obsolete. From the nineteenth century onwards, Christian Arabs – for the first time designated as such – participated in the mainstream of Arab culture. Jews did so for a while, notably in Iraq, but this came to an end with the general liquidation of the Judaeo-Arab communities.

More important and more enduring than the differences between Muslim and Christian and Jewish Arabic were the differences in language between regions and ultimately between countries. In Europe towards the end of the Middle

Ages, Latin gave way to a variety of vernaculars, which in time acquired the status of literary, governmental, and ultimately national languages. In the Middle East this did not happen. The Qur'ān, for Muslims, was the eternal, uncreated, unchanging word of God, and the language in which it was written therefore had a status enjoyed by no European language among Europeans. That status was reinforced by a vast and rich literature, covering every aspect of human endeavour, ranging from poetry and history to the most advanced scientific and philosophic writing of the time. The vernaculars seemed poor and primitive by comparison.

The implantation of Latin in much of Western Europe and the permanent Latinization, in the linguistic sense, of France, Spain and Portugal was a remarkable achievement. It was however rendered easier by the fact that there was no previous advanced or written civilization in these countries. The same may be said, with the exceptions of Mexico and Peru, of the later implantation of Spanish and Portuguese in Central and South America. But these achievements pale into insignificance in comparison with the Arabization of Southwest Asia and Northern Africa. These were regions of ancient, advanced and deep-rooted civilizations. The total and final obliteration of these civilizations and their replacement by Arab Islam must rank as one of the most successful cultural revolutions in human history.

Both the Latinized peoples of Western Europe and the Arabized peoples of the Middle East for long retained, or tried to retain, the classical languages of their former imperial masters as the media of government and commerce, religion and law, literature and science. Unlike the peoples of Western Europe, who threw off the bonds of bad Latin and raised their vernaculars to the level of literary languages, the peoples of the Middle East are still hampered by the constraints of diglossy and of an increasingly archaic and artificial medium of communication. There were some attempts to escape – the late eighteenth century Egyptian historian al-Jabartī wrote in a language which, while remaining in form literary Arabic, acquired some of the vigour and vitality of the spoken language. But this promising start was stifled by the neo-classicists of the Arab revival in the nineteenth century and after. For them, this was not living Arabic; it was just incorrect Arabic. Literary neo-classicism acquired a political dimension with the rise of pan-Arab nationalism in the twentieth century. If the Egyptians, the Syrians, the Iraqis and the rest were to develop their vernaculars into national languages, as the Spaniards, the Italians and the rest had done in Europe, then all hope of a greater Arab unity would be finally lost.

The various Arabic vernaculars, as well as the common written language, are all called Arabic – rather as if the same name 'Latin' had been used in Europe to denote the Latin of ancient Rome, of the medieval church and chanceries, of the Renaissance humanists, and, in addition, French, Spanish, Italian, and all the other modern languages of Latin origin.

West of Iran, from Iraq all the way to the Atlantic, only two language groups continued to be widely spoken despite the almost universal triumph of Arabic. They are Berber in Morocco, Algeria, Tunisia and Libya, with smaller groups in Mauritania, Sahara and Mali and one oasis in Egypt; Kurdish in Iraq, Iran, and Turkey, with smaller groups in Syria and the three Transcaucasian republics. None of these languages has official status; none has achieved a common, standard, written language. In the past, their writers expressed themselves in Arabic, Persian or Turkish; their soldiers and statesmen made their careers in predominantly Arab, Persian and Turkish armies and states. But today the speakers of these languages have become increasingly conscious of a shared and distinctive ethnic identity. Some have put forward claims ranging from cultural recognition to separate independence.

The Iranians, possessors of an ancient written culture, did not lose their language or cultural identity. Though they adopted Arabic as the language of religion and law, of culture and science, and contributed mightily to Arab culture, they did not become Arabic speakers; nor did they become Arabs as did their Western neighbours. They retained their language and their identity, albeit in a different form. The change from Zoroastrian to Islamic Persian offers interesting parallels to the transition from Anglo-Saxon to Middle English after the Norman Conquest of England. Persian was now written in the Arabic script, not in the older *pahlavi* script, which was preserved only by the Zoroastrians. It also underwent major grammatical and still more lexical changes. Its grammar, like Anglo-Saxon grammar, was broken down and simplified under the impact of conquerors who spoke another language. Its intellectual and spiritual vocabulary was almost entirely Arabic, rather like the French and classical vocabulary of post-Conquest English. But it was still Persian. It was not Arabic, and did not even belong to the same family of languages as Arabic.

Among the Muslims of Iran, Arabic was for a long time retained as the language of scripture, theology and jurisprudence, but it was replaced by neo-Persian as the medium of literature and the instrument of government. In time Persian joined Arabic as the second major classical language of Islamic civilization, especially in the Turkish lands, both Ottoman and Central Asian, among the Muslims of India, and beyond.

If Arabic was the language of religion and law, and Persian the language of love and of polite letters, Turkish soon became the language of command and of rule. The Turks, like the Arabs and unlike the Persians, came into the region from outside, from Central Asia and beyond. Like the Persians, the Turks too had their older literature, written in older scripts. Like other converts to Islam, they abandoned their older writing, and adopted the alphabet of the Qur'ān, along with a considerable vocabulary of Arabic and now also of Persian words. The Turks too had many vernaculars, most of which they did not reduce to writing. But since their language was free from the constraints of sanctity, they evolved several different written languages. The most important of these were Ottoman, Azeri, used in

Azerbaijan, Tatar, and the literary Turkish of Central Asia, variously known as Turki and Chaghatay. All these were written in the Arabic script. Under Soviet rule, the Arabic script was abolished, and replaced first by the Latin and then by a modified form of the Russian alphabet. Chaghatay, the common literary idiom, was also in effect abolished, and each people was presented with a written language based on its own vernacular, and with it, a separate locally-based national identity. Languages of the Turkic family, with a greater or lesser degree of resemblance to the Turkish of Turkey, are used in five former Soviet republics, as well as by the Tatars, Bashkirs, and other peoples within the Russian federation. There are also significant populations of speakers of Turkic languages in Iran, Afghanistan, and the Chinese People's Republic.

Apart from Iran, Persian has official status in two other countries; in Afghanistan, where the local form of Persian is known as Dari, and in the former Soviet republic of Tajikistan. Dari is written in the Perso-Arabic script and is a slightly archaic regional version of the Persian language. Tajik has been shaped by a different historical experience. Originally simply a form of Persian, written in the same script, it was, so to speak, de-Persianized by the Soviet authorities who, using the same method as with the Turkic languages, established a standard form based on local dialects and wrote it first in the Latin and then in the Cyrillic scripts.

Literary Arabic is now an official language in more than twenty states in the Middle East and North Africa. In all the Arab states it is the sole official language. In Israel, it is established, with Hebrew, as one of the two languages of the state. In Turkey and Iran, though both have significant Arabic-speaking minorities, Arabic does not have official status.

Nor do any of the numerous Arab vernaculars. In principle, literary, including broadcast Arabic, is the same from Morocco to the frontiers of Iran. Naturally there are some differences of usage, but these are no greater than between the various members of the other two great communities of language, the English-speaking and the Spanish-speaking worlds. If present trends continue, it seems likely that the speakers of Arabic will follow the example set by these two – a community of language, culture, heritage, and in large measure, religion, but no common national identity. It is, however, always possible that conflicts in places where Arabs and non-Arabs meet might stimulate greater Arab solidarity, and perhaps a resurgence of pan-Arab aspirations.

FOUR

Country

In the modern Middle East the word *watan*, along with its various derivatives and equivalents, has acquired all the political and emotional content of country, *patrie*, *Vaterland* and the rest. It figures in the names of innumerable political parties, clubs, associations and even banks; it has inspired a vast literature of poetry and polemic; it throbs in a dozen national anthems. In earlier times, with the simple meaning of home or homeland, it could have many sentimental associations, and there is no lack of poetic expressions of the love and devotion which people feel for their birthplace or homeland. More often than not, the *watan* in classical literature is a town or even a neighbourhood, a province or even a village, rather than a country in the modern sense. *Watan* might evoke affection and nostalgia; it is often linked with regrets for vanished youth, lost friends, a distant home. A tradition of dubious authenticity even quotes the Prophet himself as saying that 'love of one's country is part of the faith'. But such sentiments had no political connotation, and politically, a *watan* was merely a place. On the contrary, a political connotation is explicitly rejected and is seen as belittling. The caliph Umar is quoted as saying to the Arabs: 'Learn your genealogies, and don't be like the natives of Mesopotamia who, if asked about their origin, reply: "I come from such and such a village".'[1] In other words, descent is what honourably defines identity, not being a peasant tied to a village.

The nobility of fighting or dying for one's country – περι πατρις, *pro patria* – is familiar to Westerners from Homer and Horace and a thousand poets and orators from all over Europe. It was unknown in the Islamic world until the ideas of the French Revolution – de-Christianized and therefore admissible – brought the first real intellectual and ideological impact from Europe onto the Islamic world.

Until then, the idea of the nation or the national homeland as the basis of political identity and sovereignty was unknown to most Middle Easterners, who defined neither their own cause nor that of their enemies in terms of country. There was of course a natural attachment to the land of one's birth; local pride and rivalry are as familiar in Islamic as in Western literature, but they carried no political message. Few countries in the world can have as distinctive a character, as distinguished a history as Egypt, and Egyptian writers throughout the Muslim period take a natural pride in the glories and beauties of their homeland. But they knew little and cared less about their ignorant, pagan ancestors who lived before the coming of Islam.

This difference between Christian and Muslim usage can be seen most clearly in titulature and historiography. English or French monarchs reigned as kings of England or of France, and their historians wrote the histories of these countries. Muslim dynasts proclaimed themselves rulers of the believers, and their historians wrote of dynasties and empires or, on a smaller scale, of cities and provinces. When, in the sixteenth century, the Sultan of Turkey and the Shah of Persia exchanged abusive letters as a preliminary to war, neither called himself by such titles, but each used them to belittle his rival. Each in his own titulature was the sole legitimate sovereign of Islam; the other was a petty local potentate. Only in the nineteenth and twentieth centuries, under European influence and sometimes pressure, did Muslim rulers begin to describe their rulerships in national or territorial, that is to say in Western, terms.

At first sight, the political map of the Middle East or, as it used to be called, the Near East, looks very much like that of any other region. It consists of lines drawn across the map, enclosing territories which are called countries or – following the modern usage – nations, each of which has its own distinctive name and is the seat of a separate government ruling an independent sovereign state.

But if we look more closely, and compare the political map of the Middle East with that of, say, Europe, certain significant differences emerge. Of the twenty-five or so states that make up the map of Europe, all but a few small exceptions, such as Belgium, Switzerland and now Cyprus, have one important characteristic in common. The name of the country or nation is also the name of the dominant – sometimes the sole – ethnic group; it is also the name of the principal language used in that country, sometimes indeed only in that country. Czechoslovakia and Yugoslavia were only apparent exceptions, since these were modern names for old-established national and cultural entities. Both have since broken up – Czechoslovakia into Czech and Slovak states, Yugoslavia into its ethno-religious components.

This European combination of ethnic, territorial and linguistic nomenclature has existed for many centuries. Some of these countries, like England, France, Sweden or Spain, attained national unity and sovereignty centuries ago; but even many which did not become sovereign states had names, languages and cultures of their own, and a strong sense of territorial and national identity expressed in the cult of national history and the pursuit of national aims. In a few cases, such as Finland, Hungary, Greece and notably, Germany, the names by which they are known abroad are not the same as those which they use themselves, but the use of the same term for country, nation and language remains. Even some of the smallest of these European political entities, such as Albania and Malta, have their own national languages, known in English as Albanian and Maltese. So essential is this feature of the European pattern of identity, that even those nations which, like the Irish or the Norwegians, became accustomed during centuries of alien domination to use languages other than their own, have in modern times made great efforts to recover or reconstitute their lost national idioms.

In modern times, the European powers imposed their authority, and with it their parochial habits, on the rest of the world, in a process which extended beyond the limits of European imperial domination, and often survived its ending. One of these habits was demarcating frontiers and drawing lines on maps. In the course of the nineteenth and early twentieth centuries, first America and then most of Asia and Africa were divided, demarcated, and often renamed, until the map of all the world conformed, at least in appearance, to the European pattern.

But that appearance was often deceptive. Of the countries that appear on the map of the present-day Middle East, only three conform to the European convergence of nation, country and language; the republic of Turkey, which is inhabited by Turks who speak Turkish; Arabia, inhabited by Arabs who speak Arabic; and Iran, which in the West used to be called Persia, inhabited by Persians who speak Persian. However, the by now general acceptance of the name Iran would appear to have changed this, since Iranian is the name of the larger language family to which Persian belongs and cannot correctly be applied to the national language of Iran.

But if we look at these three more closely, we find some curious features. The name 'Turkey', as noted above, was not adopted by the Turks themselves as the official name of their homeland and state until 1923. Before the final adoption of this name, there was some disagreement about the correct form and spelling of what was then still an unfamiliar term. The form finally adopted – *Türkiye* –

clearly reveals the European origin of the name. If Turkish has borrowed and adapted a term for Turkey, Arabic still has no word for Arabia. There are of course words for 'Arab', both as adjective and as substantive, and for Arabic as a language, but no territorial designation corresponding to 'Arabia'. Present day Arabic usage resorts to such circumlocutions as the land or peninsula of the Arabs, or the Arabian land or kingdom. Both words, Turkey and Arabia, as the names of sovereign states identified by their Turkishness or their Arabness, were adopted by their own rulers and inhabitants only in the twentieth century.

This brings us to another point of dissimilarity. In Europe the names, and for the most part the entities which they designate, are old, with a continuous history dating back at least to the Middle Ages and sometimes to antiquity. This is true even of those countries which, like Germany and Italy, did not attain political unity until the nineteenth century, or those others, like Poland and the Baltic states, which did not recover or attain independence until the twentieth. The lines on the map – many of them, as in much of North America, obviously drawn with a ruler – which divide the present day Middle East into sovereign states are, with few exceptions, new. And some of the entities which they designate are new, without precedent in the medieval or ancient past.

The difference in the character of the names themselves is even more remarkable. The names by which the European states are known derive from their own languages and from their own history, and designate continuing and self-conscious entities. The names on the map of the modern Middle East are, with few exceptions, restorations or reconstructions of ancient names, a surprisingly high proportion of them of alien origin. Some of these names belong to classical antiquity. Syria and Libya are both terms of disputed etymology, which first appear in that form in Greek historical and geographical writings, and were adopted by the Roman administration as the names of provinces. From the time of the Arab conquest in the seventh century both names were virtually unknown in these and the surrounding countries, and did not reappear until they were reintroduced as a result of the spread of Western influence. The name 'Syria' came into local use, principally among non-Muslims, in the nineteenth century and designated the entire area between Taurus and Sinai, between the desert and the sea. The term 'Syrians' was widely used in the United States to designate immigrants, mostly Christians, from this area. 'Syria', in the form 'Sūriya', was adopted by the Ottomans in 1864 as the name of the province of Damascus, and became the official name of a state for the first time under the French Mandate. The republic established in the territory defined by the French Mandate was the first sovereign state ever to use the name 'Syria', and its persistence in a light Arabic disguise at the present day attests the continuing power of European modes of thought even in so intimate a matter as national identity.

The case of Libya is more dramatic. Apparently cognate names occur both in the Hebrew Bible (II Chronicles 12:3, 6:8; Nahum 3:9; Daniel 11:43) and in ancient Egyptian inscriptions, and designate peoples adjoining Egypt. The ancient Greeks adopted it, in the forms Λιβύη and Λιβύα, as the name of the southern continent in their tripartite division of the world into Europe, Asia in the East and Libya in the South. In Roman usage, Libya was replaced by Africa in this larger sense, but remained as the name of a province. Apart from a few references in Greek-based geographical writings, it disappeared entirely from Arabic usage. Its modern use seems to date from an Italian geographical work published in 1903, and it was given official existence, for the first time since the reign of the Emperor Diocletian, by an Italian royal decree of January 1, 1934. This created a new colony, formed by the union of two Italian colonies, previously the Ottoman sanjaks of Barka (Cyrenaica) and Trablusgarp (Tripolitania), and called it Libya. It is the more noteworthy that the sovereign states which emerged after the ending of French and Italian rule should have opted to retain these names, in place of those current in earlier Arabic usage.

An even more notable case is that of Palestine, a name which in its present form derives from Greek usage. It became an administrative term in Roman times. As the ending 'ine' indicates, the word was originally an adjective, not a substantive, and was used in apposition to Syria. 'Syria Palestina' was that part of southern Syria which in earlier times had been partly conquered and settled by the long vanished Philistines. Unlike Syria and Libya, the Roman name Palestine persisted into the early centuries of Arab rule, denoting a district in the province of Damascus. But it was already obsolete when the Crusaders arrived in what they called the Holy Land at the end of the eleventh century. It reappeared in Europe after the revival of classical learning associated with the Renaissance, became part of the political language of the West, though not of the region, in the nineteenth century, and was adopted by Great Britain as the name of the British mandated territory, constituted from the southernmost districts of the Ottoman provinces of Damascus and Beirut and the unattached district of Jerusalem. British imperial policy made Palestine, for the first time since the early Middle Ages, the name of a definite territory, though with frontiers quite different from those of either Roman or Arab administration, and also provided it, for the first time ever, with a 'government of Palestine'. Subsequent events, while removing this, have created a Palestinian nation.

Other names are of various patterns. Lebanon is a mountain, Jordan a river, Iraq the name of a medieval caliphal province. The pre-classical names have almost all disappeared. Israel, which alone is known by the same name, in the same language, though not with the same boundaries as in antiquity, is an apparent, not a real exception. Its presence is due not to a survival but to a restoration after a political discontinuity of almost two millennia. Egypt is known at home and in the Islamic world by the Arabic name Misr, from an ancient Semitic noun, probably meaning a march or border province; cognate names are used in Hebrew, Aramaic, and other Semitic languages. Elsewhere the country is known by derivatives of a Greek name, Aigyptos, the second syllable of which preserves a distant echo of one of the names of ancient Egypt, the same as appears in the word Copt. But of the names by which the ancient Egyptians – and for that matter the ancient Assyrians, Babylonians, Phoenicians, Aramaeans and others – knew themselves and their countries, no trace remains except in ancient writings and in the modern scholarship which has recovered and deciphered them.

In much of this, there are obvious similarities with the situation in the Americas. There too, national, territorial, ethnic and linguistic names rarely if ever coincide, and most of the sovereign states of the continent are known by names which reflect the fantasy, the book-learning or the convenience of their former conquerors and rulers. Part of this similarity is due to common experience. In the Middle East as in the Americas and indeed in much of Africa, the positioning of the lines on the maps is a relic of the imperial age, and reflects the conflicts and compromises of the former imperial powers. Even the names applied to the territories enclosed by these lines are part of the cultural baggage of the departed imperial rulers.

But the Middle East is very different from the American continent, where, with the exception only of two areas, there were no developed civilizations, no written languages and no historical memories before the arrival of the conquistadores. The Middle East is an area of ancient civilizations, indeed, the most ancient in the world. But these ancient civilizations are dead, and were until very recently forgotten and literally buried in the ground. The advent of Islam, the adoption of the Arabic language, brought a new identity, and with it a new past, a new set of memories.

The regions into which the Middle East was divided in the classical Islamic period differ both from those of the ancient civilizations and from those of the modern state system, even where the names are the same. Egypt, of course, was always Egypt, unequivocally defined by geography and by a way of life which continued even when religion, language, and culture changed. Elsewhere, the boundaries were less certain. North Africa, which Muslims call the Maghrib, had two major centres, Ifrīqiya (from Roman Africa), that is, the present-day Tunisia, and Morocco. The countries now called Algeria and Libya were borderlands, Algeria between the Moroccan and Tunisian centres, Libya between Tunisia and Egypt. The emergence of distinctive separate entities in these two areas dates from the Ottoman period. Their modern names and boundaries are a legacy of colonialism – French in the one, Italian in the other.

In Arab southwest Asia, the Arab literary and historical tradition recognized four major areas as well as some smaller ones. The Arabic name Shām denoted the region known as Syria in Greco-Roman times. In twentieth-century terms, it comprised the whole area of Syria, Lebanon, Jordan, Palestine, and Israel, as well as some parts of what is now southern Turkey. To the northeast was Mesopotamia which the Arabs called Jazīra, in what is now northern Iraq, with parts of northeastern Syria and southeastern Turkey. South of that was the medieval Iraq, extending from Takrīt down to the Persian Gulf, with some adjoining area of Iran, in classical usage termed Iraq 'Ajami. The Arabian peninsula, as always, was infinitely subdivided. The Arab geographers speak of two main areas, the North, with its centres variously situated in Hijaz and Najd, and the South, centred on the ancient civilizations of Yemen.

Iran had a common identity only in legend and literature. For practical purposes, the land of Iran was subdivided into distinctive regions, notably Fārs, which the Greek called Persis, in the southwest, Khurāsān in the east, and Sīstān in the southeast. Other regions are usually known by the names of their chief cities or tribes. Beyond the traditional ancient boundaries of Iran – the Elburz Mountains in the north, the Oxus River in the northeast – there were new territories of Iranian settlement.

Arabic usage frequently gave the same name to a district

or province and its chief city. To this day, the same word is used for Algiers and Algeria, for Tunis and Tunisia. In classical and to some extent in modern usage Shām denotes both Syria and Damascus, Misr both Egypt and Cairo.

Although there was no city in the Greco-Roman sense, there were major urban areas that developed a strong sense of identity. Rivalries between cities are frequently expressed in literature, more often than not in a tone of light banter. Such for example are the traditional rivalries and competition between Isfahan and Shiraz in Iran, between Damascus and Aleppo in Syria, between Mosul, Baghdad and Basra in Iraq. More serious rivalries and even feuds, sometimes of long duration, could arise between neighbouring villages in the countryside, between neighbouring quarters in a city. These regional and local solidarities and hostilities continue to play a significant part in modern politics. Palestinians and Jordanians in the Hashimite Kingdom provide an obvious example. Palestine and Jordan, as denoting state entities, are both twentieth-century innovations, and were introduced in two stages, through first the establishment and then the termination of the British Mandate. Before that, both the east and west banks of Jordan were inhabited by Arabic-speaking Muslims and ruled by the same government, whether situated in Istanbul, Damascus, Cairo, or elsewhere. There were of course the usual regional differences and rivalries between east and west, as also between north and south. But in the late twentieth century the regional difference between east and west has acquired a new dimension through the very different political experiences of East Bank and West Bank Arabs.

The recovery by the peoples of the Middle East of their ancient history and eventually identity did not begin until the nineteenth century. This new interest in the more distant past was provoked by the newly-imported European idea of fatherland, of the continuing, almost mystical relationship between a people and the country they inhabit. That the recovery was possible, was due above all to two causes: the pertinacity of their own non-Muslim minorities, and the curiosity and persistence of strangers who came from Europe. At the dawn of modern history, all that Christian Europe knew about the ancient Middle East was what was contained in the writings of two peoples, active in antiquity, who had retained both their memories and their voices – the Greeks and the Jews. The Muslims, who read neither the classics nor the Bible, were even worse placed, and relied for what little they knew on Qur'anic versions of Biblical stories.

But there was in their midst another possible source of information, in religious communities as ancient and as pertinacious as the Jews and with roots going back to remote antiquity. Two in particular preserved written traditions connecting them with their ancestors; the Christian Copts of Egypt and the Zoroastrians of Iran and India. These communities held the keys which enabled European scholars to unlock the secrets of the ancient Middle Eastern past. One such was a German Jesuit called Athanasius Kircher, who died in 1680 and was the first major European scholar in the field of Coptic studies. He studied under Coptic priests, learned how to read their ancient language, compiled Coptic grammars and dictionaries, and thus took the first essential step which, generations later, made possible the decipherment of the Egyptian hieroglyphs. Another was the French philologist Anquetil Duperron, who made his way to India, sat at the feet of Parsee priests, edited and translated some of the Zoroastrian scriptures, and thus too opened the way for the decipherment, at a later date, of the ancient Iranian inscriptions.

In its origins this whole process, of what came to be known as Egyptology, Assyriology, Iranology, and other parallel disciplines in the study of the ancient Middle East, was exclusively and entirely the preoccupation of European and, later, American scholars. The discovery, care, decipherment, evaluation, and interpretation of these records of the ancient past was a non-Middle Eastern enterprise and achievement, and for a long time it had no impact on the peoples of the Islamic Middle East, who remained uninterested in their own pagan past. For them, significant history began with the advent of Islam. That was their own, their true history, the history that mattered. What came before was an age of ignorance, of no value and with no lesson to teach.

A new phase and a new attitude to the national past – an expression which for the first time now acquired a meaning in these parts – began in Egypt and spread at a later date to other Middle Eastern countries. There were several circumstances in Egypt which favoured this change. One is the very character of Egypt as a country: the green gash of the Nile, opening out into the delta with the desert on both sides. There can hardly be another country in the world, the identity and distinctiveness of which are so clearly stamped by geography as well as history. It was much easier for the Egyptians to develop a sense of Egyptian identity than for other countries where the borders, both geographical and ethnic, merge imperceptibly into those of their neighbours. Egypt also had what were probably not only the most impressive remains of antiquity, but the most accessible. In Iran one had to go to Persepolis or to Behistun, in Turkey to Bogazköy, in Iraq to Nineveh and other remote places, often involving difficult and dangerous journeys, which only Orientalists had the incentive to undertake. In Egypt some of the most impressive monuments of Pharaonic antiquity were a stone's throw from major places of habitation. They were things which people could see, had indeed grown up seeing, and the new message of patriotic pride was therefore much easier to convey.

Egypt was also, for a long time, the country in the Middle East which, apart from Turkey, was most open to European contacts and therefore to European influences, intellectual as well as political and commercial. Another factor of some relevance is that in the nineteenth century, Egypt was ruled by a nominally vassal dynasty with separatist ambitions, and therefore with a definite interest in fostering the notion of a separate Egyptian identity within the Ottoman Empire of which Egypt was then a province. In 1868 Shaykh Rifā'a Rafi' al-Tahtāwī, an Egyptian scholar who had spent some years in France, published a book on the history of Egypt from the beginnings to the Arab conquest. That is to say, his history ended where until then Arabic historiography in Egypt had begun; it covered the hitherto unknown prehistory of the country. It was an epoch-making book, not only in the development of Egyptian historiography, but also in the self-awareness of the Egyptians of themselves as a nation. This was the beginning of a process which added several thousand years to what the Egyptians knew about their own history, and it was followed by a very rapid development – the publication of many books, first translations then original works, the growth of Egyptology among the Egyptians, and a new kind of history-teaching in the schools.

It also marked the beginning of what has become a continuing tension between the two Egyptian personalities; the one Islamic, its language and culture Arabic, its history that of Islam, the other Egyptian and, so to speak, pharaonic, defining itself not in religious and communal but in national and patriotic terms. This was a new and different type of loyalty, based on a new and different sense of identity.

Obviously this dichotomy had considerable political implications. The one identity drew Egypt in the direction of pan-Arab or even pan-Islamic causes, the other towards a territorially based Western-style patriotism. The latter is often called Egyptianism or, by people in other Arab countries, pharaonism, a word used with hostile intent. The Arabic is *tafar'un*, which literally means pretending to be pharaonic.

This movement in Egypt was first opposed, condemned, even derided in other Arabic speaking countries. It was seen as something artificial, as a parochial attempt to create a little Egypt within the greater Arab or Islamic brotherhood. It was denounced by pan-Arabs as separatist, by religious people as neo-pagan, and by both as divisive. Nevertheless the example of Egypt had an impact in other Middle Eastern lands. Egypt was by far the most advanced country, intellectually, in the Arab world, with considerable influence not only among the Arabs but wherever Arabic was read, and that meant, at that time, virtually the whole Islamic world. Parallel movements developed among other peoples, often again with significant political and even territorial undertones and overtones.

A similar recovery and repossession of the past occurred in Iraq, though there it was slower and later than in Egypt. The Iraqis too could claim ancient and glorious ancestors, or at least predecessors – the Sumerians, the Assyrians, the Babylonians, who also left massive and imposing artifacts. But for a variety of reasons the development of national archeology was slower and later in Iraq than in Egypt. And when Iraqis claim the Assyrians and Babylonians as their glorious ancestors, they grant them a kind of retroactive posthumous Arab naturalization, and speak of their ancestors as ancient Arabs, rather than of themselves as modern Assyro-Babylonians. The ancient Assyrian and Babylonian language, though not Arabic, is, unlike Egyptian, of the Semitic family, and this affinity helped to soften, though not entirely to obviate, the clash of national identities and histories. Some modern Arab writers have indeed gone so far as to claim all the ancient Semitic languages as Arabic, and their speakers as Arabs. Some do the same with two exceptions – the Jews and the Ethiopians. This retroactive Arabization made possible another feature of modern nationalist historiography. If the inhabitants of Iraq, Syria, Palestine and the North African littoral were already Arabs since antiquity, then the wars conducted by the Muslim caliphate were not conquests; they were wars of liberation, waged to free their Arab brothers from Persian and Byzantine imperialist oppression.

In recent years, and particularly under the shock of the war with the Islamic Republic of Iran, the evocation of antiquity has become more common and more urgent. Iraq is a deeply divided country. Religiously, a Sunni ascendancy rules a Shī'ite majority, and the Shī'ites, though Arab, share the faith of the Persians. Ethnically, an Arab majority dominates a Kurdish minority – and the Kurdish language belongs neither to the Arabic nor the Semitic family, but is related to Persian as Portuguese is to Spanish. The concept of an ancient Iraqi nation, territorially defined, with roots reaching back to remote antiquity, could be a powerful unifying force, and it is not surprising that Iraqi leaders have had frequent recourse to it. President Saddam Hussein has often referred to Nebuchadnezzar as an Iraqi hero, commending in particular his expeditious handling of the Zionist problem in his day.

The rediscovery came still later in Iran, where Iranian intellectuals read European scholarship and literature, and began to realize that they too had an ancient and glorious past to which they could lay claim. In Iran as in Egypt, the ancient past had been forgotten and to an even greater extent obliterated. In Persepolis, the ancient Persian capital, the Muslim conquerors had hacked away the faces of the Medes and Persians depicted in the friezes, seeing in them an expression of pagan idolatry. Only the most recent pre-Islamic history, that of the Sasanid shahs who ruled Iran on the eve of the Arab conquest, was known at all, and that only in sketchy form, and from Arabic sources. The more ancient history of Iran was forgotten, and even the name of Cyrus, the founder of the Persian state, was unknown.

The first modern Iranian writings about ancient Iran appeared in the third quarter of the nineteenth century. They were still on a rather small scale and based entirely on Western sources, mostly French. Cyrus did not become a popular hero until the present century, when he became known through two historical novels in which he figured as hero, the one published in 1919, the other in 1921. The cult of antiquity in Iran reached its height under the Pahlavi dynasty, which ruled from 1925 to 1979. The information about antiquity used by modern Iranian historians and novelists was for long derived exclusively from Western sources. By the late nineteenth and early twentieth century, histories of Iran were beginning to include the ancient empires, departing for the first time from the heroic mythologies which until then had provided the only accounts of ancient Iran available in the Persian language.

The case of Iran is somewhat paradoxical. The rediscovery of antiquity in that country came rather later than in Iraq and Syria, much later than in Egypt. In modern times, it was the last of the major Middle Eastern Muslim countries to recover its memory of antiquity. And yet, after the shock of the Arab conquests, it was the first to recover some sense of separate and distinctive identity. Of all the countries of southwest Asia and North Africa conquered and Islamized by the Arabs in the seventh and eighth centuries, Iran alone retained its language and still uses it to the present day, albeit written in the Arabic script and with a large vocabulary of Arab loanwords. Persians also retained a strong awareness of their homeland as something more than just a place. Iran may not have been a coherent political entity like Egypt, still less a nation or a country in the modern sense of these words, but it was certainly an idea, an entity, conceived at first in cultural, later in political terms. The pride of the Persians in their language and in their literary traditions is familiar to any who have had dealings with them. It is expressed in particular in the great Persian epics which purport to tell the noble and heroic deeds of ancient Iran. The stories related in the *Shāhnāma*, the famous Persian book of kings, derive from a mythical, not a real history. But the myth served to buttress and to reinforce this sense of Persian national identity within the Islamic fold. And later, it helped and was helped by the emergence of separate states in Iran, ruled by Muslim but Iranian dynasties, with courts that became centres of Persian culture.

It is not difficult to see reasons why the Persians, though they adopted Islam with as great enthusiasm as any other Muslim people, nevertheless did not adopt an Arab identity. The Arabs conquered Iran not from another alien ruler, but from a great Iranian empire, that of the Sasanid shahs. And the Iranians, unlike their neighbours to the west, were still sustained by fresh and recent memories of independence and greatness. The countries west of Iran – Iraq, Syria, Palestine, Egypt, North Africa – were all long subjugated provinces of distant empires, and had undergone many changes of government, law, religion, culture, and even language. The process of eradicating the ancient past was already far advanced when the Arabs arrived.

None of this had happened in Iran, and it was therefore not surprising that, after a century or two of Arab-Muslim rule, there was a cultural awakening – a revival of the Persian language, and the emergence of a new Persian national culture, deeply influenced by Arabic and imbued with the spirit of Islam, but nevertheless unmistakably Persian, and differing from Arab Islam in several significant respects. In the Persian literature of the time, and even in Arabic literature written by Persians, there is an awareness of difference, a sense of historic and cultural identity. Persian poets speak with pride of their double inheritance, the religion of Muhammad and the glory of Chosroes and of the by now mythical heroes of ancient Iran. Sometimes they even dare to assert their own superiority over their upstart conquerors. This was a process which had no parallel elsewhere in the Middle Eastern and North African Islamic world, until the coming of the Turks.

The Turkish case is very different from that of other peoples of the region. The Turks came into the Middle East from Central Asia, where they had already embraced Islam, and their conquest and settlement of the country which came to be known as Turkey dated only from the eleventh century. Until their arrival, the country was predominantly Greek in language and culture and Christian in religion, and any attempt to identify with these, in the age of archeological self-rediscovery, was clearly impossible. The modern, nationalist Turks therefore looked beyond the Greek colonists of Asia Minor to the ancient inhabitants of the peninsula, and saw themselves as the successors of the pre-Hellenic Anatolian peoples, notably the Hittites.

The Palestinian Arabs confronted the same problem in a more acute form. Had the Jews disappeared like most of the peoples of antiquity, the Palestinians might have claimed to be the heirs of ancient Israel, as the Egyptians were of the pharaohs and the Iraqis of the kings of Babylon. But the Jews had not disappeared and were even returning, and the Palestinians therefore sought their legitimacy in the pre-Israelite inhabitants of Palestine, the Canaanites. In Syria the survival of Aramaic Christianity presented the same problem in a much milder form. At one time Aramaic culture was particularly associated with the Christian minority and even with the Christian-led Syrian Popular Party, to such a point that any reference to Aramaic culture was seen as a politically seditious act. That phase appears to have passed, and the Aramaeans are now acceptable as legitimate ancestors of modern Syria.

In Lebanon there was for a while a tendency among some Lebanese, vehemently opposed by other Lebanese, to identify with the ancient Phoenicians who had lived along that strip of the Levant coast. This view was to be found principally among Christians, more particularly among westward looking Maronite Christians, who saw in it a way of differentiating themselves from their Arab and Islamic neighbours. It commands very little support at the present time. The Phoenician settlers in North Africa however, who founded the city and civilization of Carthage, have been adopted as both Arabs and ancestors in Tunisia and to some extent in Algeria. These arguments are in no way impeded by the fact that the Carthaginian, Phoenician and Canaanite languages belong to the same subgroup of Semitic as Hebrew.

The idea of a profound and unending linkage between a people and the country they inhabit, continuing through changes of culture, language and even religion, was alien and difficult to accept. But it has made remarkable headway, and has appeared in unexpected places. In 1971, when the Shah of Iran held a great celebration in Persepolis to commemorate the 2,500th anniversary of the foundation of the Persian monarchy by Cyrus the Great, he was vehemently attacked on Islamic religious grounds. Exalting the monarchy was bad enough, but far worse was the proclamation of a common identity with the pagan past, and a consequent redefinition of the basis of allegiance. For the Shah's religious critics, the identity of Iranians was defined by Islam, and their brothers were Muslims in other countries, not their own unbelieving and misguided ancestors. The Islamic revolution brought interesting variations on this theme.

In the mid-nineteenth century, an Arabic-speaking Christian of the Greek Orthodox Church in Damascus would have identified himself, in different situations, as a subject of the Ottoman State and as a member of the Greek Orthodox Church. If some regional definition was needed, he would have called himself a Damascene. If he knew a Western language and was familiar with Western writings, he might even have called himself a Syrian, though this is unlikely. Though he spoke Arabic, he would in no circumstances have called himself an Arab. Since then, his situation has changed radically. His passport, if he has one, will describe him as Syrian – not, as previously, a subject of a pluralistic polyglot Empire, but a citizen of a national state officially described as the 'Syrian Arab Republic'. By religion he is Orthodox, a member of a purely religious minority, enjoying full theoretical equality with the majority and therefore retaining no *dhimmi* exemptions or immunities. By language and culture he is an Arab, with a strong – but variously defined – sense of common identity with people in other countries who share the same language and culture.

Even in Egypt – by far the most homogeneous and unified of the Arabic-speaking countries – there are also different levels of identity. A Cairene Muslim may, in different situations, see himself as an Egyptian, proud of the multi-millennial glory of his country, with a history dating back to the Pharaohs of antiquity; as an Arab, claiming a common identity with all those who share the Arabic language and culture irrespective of country, race or religion; or as a Muslim, for whom other Muslims as far away as Bangladesh and Indonesia are brothers while his Coptic next-door neighbours – unquestionably Egyptian by origin, and Arab by language and culture, but Christian – are not. The modern history of Egypt reflects the interaction of these different identities and the waxing and waning of the different ideologies that they inspire.

In other countries of greater diversity, identities are correspondingly more complex. In the kingdom, later the Republic of Iraq, one of the successor states of the Ottoman Empire, a citizen might define himself by region. Mosul, Baghdad and Basra, the three Ottoman vilayets from which the new state of Iraq was composed, have old, pertinaceous and distinctive local traditions. He might do so by ethnicity, Arab or Kurdish, the latter with local roots dating back to pre-Islamic times, the former with ties, at least of sentiment, to other Arab countries; or by religion, Muslim or Christian, the former split into Sunni and Shī'a, the latter into Nestorians and Uniates. The Jewish minority has virtually disappeared.

The Palestinian's choice was at once more stark and less clear. The Palestine Mandate, like those for Iraq and Syria, was fashioned from former Ottoman provinces, with frontiers determined by the mandatory powers, acting jointly or alone. Like Syria, and unlike Iraq, the Palestine Mandate was subdivided. In Syria the French created a separate republic of Lebanon, including the old autonomous region of the mountain with some additional districts; they retained the name Syria for the remainder. In Palestine, the British separated transjordanian Palestine, which became an Arab emirate, later monarchy, known as Transjordan and then Jordan, and retained the name Palestine for the cisjordanian districts. The subsequent difference between 'Palestinian' and 'Jordanian' is historical and ideological, rather than national or geographical. Both Filastin and Urdunn designated provinces in the early Arab period, corresponding to the late Roman Palestina Prima and Palestina Secunda, but both extended from the sea to the desert, and the boundary (not frontier) between them was horizontal not vertical. In this century, both names have been used on both sides of the River Jordan. Since the end of the British Mandate in 1948, the Jordanian identity has meant allegiance to the Hashimite monarchy; the name Palestinian has connoted the demand for a Palestinian state – for some next to Israel, for others, in its place. Today the differences between Jordanians and Palestinians are a compound of old-fashioned regional particularism, recent and current experience, and ideological and political choices.

Sometimes the recovery of different pasts can produce clashes of loyalty and even identity. Until the findings of Egyptology became known to them, all that most Egyptians knew about Pharaoh was what they learnt from the Qur'an, and the image of Pharaoh in the Qur'an is much the same as in the Old Testament. For Muslims as for Christians and Jews, Pharaoh was the archetypal pagan tyrant and oppressor, the villain of a story in which the heroes are the Banū Isrā'īl, the children of Israel. But the incorporation of Egyptological findings in Egyptian school histories gave the average Egyptian a new image of Pharaoh – the protagonist of the great and glorious ancient past of his country, a source of legitimate national pride. The two images – Pharaoh of the schoolbook, and Pharaoh of the Qur'ān – are obviously irreconcilable, and the tension became greater when Egyptians found themselves at war with the present-day children of Israel. For the pious Muslim, the Banū Isrā'īl of the Qur'ānic Exodus story have little or nothing to do with the Jews, known by that name in the time of the Prophet as at the present time. The Banū Isrā'īl were the followers of the Prophet Moses, one of the many precursors of the Prophet Muhammad; they were thus part of the sequence of revelations that constitutes Islam, of which the mission of Muhammad represented the final completion. When the devout assassin of President Sadat proudly proclaimed, 'I have killed Pharaoh' he was obviously referring to the Pharaoh of traditional religious literature, and not of the new Egyptian patriotism. The tension between Egypt's different pasts remains.

Sometimes the problem is not one country with two pasts, but one past claimed by two countries. During the Iraq–Iran War 1980–1988, the propaganda of both sides made frequent reference to the Battle of Qādisiyya, fought in 636 or 637 CE. The precise date is disputed in the original sources; so, at the present time, is the significance of the battle. There is general agreement on the course of events. An Arab Muslim army, coming out of Arabia, encountered the army of Sasanid Shah, and won an overwhelming victory, opening the way to the conquest and Islamization of Persia. For Saddam Hussein, this was a great victory of Arabs over Persians, and a source of national pride and encouragement to the Iraqis in their war against Iran. For the Iranians, it did not matter that the Muslims were Arabs and the infidels were Persians. Qādisiyya was a blessed event, a triumph of the true faith over unbelief, preparing the way for the Islamization of Iran and its peoples. Both sides therefore could legitimately and honourably claim Qādisiyya as a victory, depending on how they identified the parties in that ancient battle, and the parties in the modern war.

The war between Iraq and Iran demonstrated in an interesting way the insufficiency of both ethnic and sectarian appeals and perhaps also the power of patriotic loyalty. When the Iraqis invaded Iran, they hoped that the large Arabic-speaking population of the Iranian province of Khuzistan would welcome them. They did not, but remained faithful to their Iranian allegiance. When the Iranians in turn counterattacked, they hoped that the large Shī'ite population of Iraq would rally to the cause of the Shī'ite Islamic Republic. Some of them indeed did so, but the vast majority of Iraqi Shī'ites remain loyal to their country.

All over the Middle East, not only in old nations like Iran and Egypt, but even in some of the newest and most artificial, the state is once again becoming the primary focus of political loyalty and identity. Like South America, which it in some ways resembles, the Arab world consists of a large number of separate states. These states have a great deal in common – in language and culture, religion and society, history and destiny. As in South America, there was a moment, after the crumbling of empires, when they might have fashioned a greater unity. They did not, and the moment passed. In language and culture, the growth of literacy and the improvement of communication will no doubt bring greater unity. In politics, it would seem that their destiny is one of separate political statehood, becoming nationhood. The lines which colonial soldiers and administrators and imperial diplomats drew on the map of the Middle East and North Africa have hardened, and their power to enclose and to divide is likely to endure for some time to come.

FIVE

Nation

The word 'nation', even in English, has gone through a number of substantial changes. The first of several definitions in the Oxford English Dictionary explains it as 'a distinct race or people, characterized by common descent, language, or history, usually organized as a separate political state and occupying a definite territory'. It was not always so in the past; it has not always remained so in the present. In the medieval universities, the 'nations' were the quarters in which students of various origins were lodged, according to their places of origin. These might include provinces within the same country. In modern American usage, nation has acquired an unmistakable connotation of territory and sovereignty. It is in this sense that the word nation is used in the 'League of Nations' and the 'United Nations'. A newly independent state, irrespective of how it is constituted and how ancient its national identity, may be described as a 'new nation'. Americans planning to travel by car from New York to California will even speak of 'driving across the nation', an expression that to English ears suggests the massive ill-treatment of large numbers of people.

In the Western world, the idea has gradually been accepted and established that nationhood and statehood are or should be identical, that loyalty to the nation and allegiance to the state should coincide, and that if they do not this is a fault which should be remedied. According to predominant modern opinion, a nation which has not expressed its nationhood in statehood is somehow deprived; a state which is not national, which is merely dynastic or imperial, is fundamentally flawed and ultimately doomed.

For the purposes of this discussion, the term nation is used without its connotations of territory or sovereign statehood. In this sense, a nation means a group of people held together by a common language, belief in a common descent and in a shared history and destiny. They usually but do not necessarily inhabit a contiguous territory; they often enjoy, and if they do not enjoy they commonly seek, sovereign independence in their own name. This definition will make it easier to understand the evolution of nationhood among the peoples of the Middle East. For this purpose, it may be helpful to examine Middle Eastern terms.

The Hebrew Bible commonly uses four words, which in various contexts may be translated as nation or people: *lĕom*, *umma*, *'am*, and *goy*. All four are used in the sense both of nation and of people; all four, including the last, are used both of the Jews and of their neighbours. Thus in the well-known passage in Exodus 19:6, in which the children of Israel are told that they will be 'a kingdom of priests and an holy nation', the word translated nation is *goy*. In later usage, the plural form *goyim* came to mean the nations other than Israel, hence gentiles – a word that has undergone a parallel semantic evolution. In modern Hebrew *lĕom* has given rise to *lĕumi*, national, as in *Bank Lĕumi*, (national bank) and even *lĕumanut*, nationalism. These are of course loan translations of Western terms. On the identity cards all Israelis are required to carry, there are two lines defining identity, in both Hebrew and Arabic, the two official languages of the state. The first is citizenship (Hebrew *ezrahūt*, Arabic *jinsiyya*), which for all citizens of the state is the same, namely Israeli. The other, denoted by the Hebrew *lĕom* and the Arabic *qawmiyya*, is clearly intended to mean ethnic nationality, the usual answers, for the vast majority of Israeli citizens, being Jewish or Arab.

The term *qawmiyya* is now widely used in Arabic, with a connotation of ethnic nationality or nationalism, particularly in the pan-Arab sense. It is however a word of fairly recent origin, and has already undergone several changes of meaning. The classical Arabic terms denoting group identity are *umma* and *milla*. Both have their analogs in Hebrew and Aramaic, and are very likely loanwords from those languages. Both occur in the Qur'ān. *Umma* seems to mean no more than a group of people, however defined – by descent, by language, by creed, by conduct, or other. It may refer to whole communities, or to subgroups within such communities, as for example, the righteous (3:109ff; 5:70; 7:159). In some passages it is even applied to the *Jinn* or genies (Qur'ān 7:36; 41:24; 46:17), and, in one passage (6:38) to all living creatures. With the advent of Islam, the *umma* of the Arabs became the *umma* of Muhammad, a religiously defined community from which unbelieving Arabs were excluded, and which non-Arabs could join by conversion. In this usage of the term, the Jews, Christians and others each had their own *umma*.

Despite this generally accepted religious re-definition, *umma* also remained in use in the older, ethnic sense. There are many passages in classical Arabic comparing the merits and defects of different '*ummas*'. The groups discussed are sometimes ethnic: Arabs, Persians and Turks, Indians and Chinese, Africans and Europeans; sometimes religious: Jews, Christians, Zoroastrians. Often the writer's intention is not clear, perhaps not even to himself. In speaking of 'the Persians', does he mean followers of the old Persian religion, or does he include Muslim Persians of his own time? In speaking of Arabs, does he include Christians? These questions have been differently answered. In Persian and Turkish, which adopted the term *umma* along with many other Qur'ānic terms, the word retained a purely religious connotation, and is little used at the present time. In modern Arabic, it has recovered its previous national connotation and is used, especially in nationalist discourse, of the greater Arab nation, without distinction of country or creed. But the religious connotation remains, primarily but not exclusively in religious discourse, with the inevitable resulting ambiguities.

The word *milla* seems to have moved in the opposite direction. It occurs frequently in the Hebrew Bible, with the meaning of 'word' or 'utterance'. In the forms *milta* or *mellta*, it is used in ancient Jewish and Christian Aramaic texts in the same sense. In some Christian texts it appears as the equivalent of the Greek *logos*. In the Qur'ān it denotes a religious group, perhaps in the sense of those who follow the word of God in a certain way. These include Jews, Christians, adherents of other ancient prophets, and even heathens. It is used more particularly of the 'religion of Abraham' (*millat Ibrāhīm*) founded by the patriarch, renewed by several successive prophets, and brought to its final perfection by the prophet Muhammad. In classical Arabic usage the word meant a religious community, primarily but not exclusively that of Islam. At the present time *milla* is no longer in current use in Arabic.

In Persian and Turkish, which adopted it along with other Arabic terms, the word has in modern usage taken on entirely new meanings. The Persian *millat* and Turkish *millet* were for long used in the Qur'ānic sense of a religious community. In the Ottoman Empire it was indeed the technical term applied to the officially recognized religious communities, consisting of the Muslims, sometimes known as the 'ruling millet' (*millet-i hākime*), the Orthodox, the Armenians, and the Jews. Later some other Christian denominations were added. The word was used in a similar sense in Iran. But with the advent of modern nationalist ideas in both countries, *millet*, significantly, was the word adopted to denote the nation, with *millī* as national, *milliyet* as nationalism, and, in Turkish, *milliyetçi* as nationalist. In late Ottoman usage, the term *beyn elmilel* (i.e. between the millets) was adopted as equivalent of the Western term 'international'. It has been replaced in modern Turkish by *uluslararasi*, from *ulus*, an altaic term for a large tribe.

Discussions of ethnicity in classical Middle Eastern literature are usually in the context of origin or employment – that is, of tribes or slaves. Often the two are linked since many of the slaves are identified by their tribes of origin. Most of the discussions of ethnic categories and differences occur in what one might call consumer-guides for purchasers of slaves. There is a fairly extensive literature of such manuals, which discuss the slaves according to their different ethnic origins, the merits and defects of each group, and their various aptitudes for the three main functions of the slave – as servant, concubine, and soldier.

Ethnic differences are also mentioned in the context of rivalries within the military and sometimes, though less frequently, the civil service establishments. Thus, for example, at the court of the Fatimid caliphs in medieval Cairo, there are reports of ongoing rivalries and clashes between whites and blacks, Turks and Berbers, and feuding groups within each of these. Similarly, in the Ottoman establishment, there were rivalries and clashes between Balkan and Caucasian slaves, and between the different components of each group. Remnants of these groups – Bosniaks and Albanians from Europe, Georgians and Circassians from the Caucasus – may still be traced in the modern republic of Turkey, where, if Muslim, they are all regarded as Turks.

The introduction of alien nationalist ideologies, and more particularly the recycling of venerable religious terms with a new nationalist, and by implication non-religious, meaning, did not fail to arouse opposition among those who saw these new ideas as divisive and destructive. Ironically, the term *qawmiyya*, in its Turkish form *kavmiyet*, appears to have been first coined and used by Turkish anti-nationalists with an unmistakably negative sense of tribal or factional loyalties. The nineteenth-century Ottomans used their scriptural and classical languages, Arabic and Persian, as a quarry of lexical raw materials, in much the same way as the West used Latin and Greek; in so doing they created many Arabic and Persian words unknown to the Arabs and Persians. Some of these were repossessed; sometimes, like *qawmiyya*, with an abrupt change of meaning.

While *qawmiyya* in modern Arabic has a positive connotation, other terms are used by supporters of greater Arab unity to condemn regional and sectional identities. One such is *'asabiyya*, in earlier times a positive term for tribal or ethnic solidarity. The more usual term of abuse is *shu'ū biyya*, from *shu'ūb*, the plural of *sha'b*, meaning 'people'. *Sha'b* in Arabic is positive, and often has a populist rather than a nationalist content. It acquired the latter meaning during the struggle in the late nineteenth and twentieth centuries against foreign occupation and domination. These struggles were necessarily regional, and the term therefore acquired a regional content, being used of the Egyptian *sha'b*, the Syrian *sha'b*, the Palestinian *sha'b*, etc., rather than of the Arabs as a whole. More recently, the term *sha'b* has come to be used in a socio-economic sense, to denote the mass of the common people. *Shu'ūbiyya*, in contrast, is and has always been unequivocally negative. In medieval usage, it denoted the attempt by the conquered peoples, especially the Persians, to reassert their national identity and reclaim their national dignity against Arab domination. In modern times, it has been revived to denote what are seen as separatist or local tendencies in the various Arab countries, as against the greater unity of the Arabs as a whole.

In its national identities, as in so much else, the Middle East displays a pattern of discontinuity and diversity. The Bible has preserved the names and some elements of the history of many nations, great and small, who lived in the region in antiquity. The recovery and decipherment, in modern times, of other ancient Middle Eastern texts have added new names, and increased our knowledge of the old. Some of these names, like Babylon and Assyria, Egypt and Persia, are places, the homes of peoples who founded states, some of them long-lived, and conquered empires. Some of them were tribes, named after some eponymous ancestor. They roved the deserts and steppes of the Middle East, and such states or principalities as they formed were mostly ephemeral. Such were the Jebusites, Amalekites and Ammonites.

Such too were the Israelites or Benê Israel, the children of Israel. Israel was the by-name of the patriarch Jacob, father of twelve sons who founded the twelve tribes. The name of one of them, Judah, is the source both of the Roman place name Judaea and the modern term 'Jew' denoting a follower of the Jewish religion. Significantly, the term 'Judaism' does not appear in any Hebrew text until the eleventh century CE, when it is used by a rabbinical commentator in France. The term first appears in Greek, in the form *ioudaismos*, in the book of Maccabees. From the content it is clear that it means 'Jewishness', a Jewish way of life, rather than the name of a religion. In this it parallels the earliest usage of the term Christianity – Greek *Christianismos* – in the sense of a Christian way of life.

Only a very few of the other nations named in the Old Testament survived as national entities through medieval into modern times. Of these, far and away the most important are the inter-related groups of people known as Arab. This name occurs several times in the Hebrew Bible as well as in other ancient and classical texts. Sometimes it appears as a toponym, referring to the Arabian peninsula or to its northern regions. More often it refers to the tribal peoples living on the desert borderlands of Iraq, Syria and Palestine, but not to the inhabitants of these countries. The earliest dated occurrence of the name is in an Assyrian inscription of the mid-ninth century BCE, recording an Assyrian victory over a conspiracy of rebel chieftains, one of them named as 'Gindibu the Aribi'. Thereafter there are frequent references in ancient inscriptions, usually recording the receipt of tribute from the border chieftains, or the dispatch of punitive expeditions when they caused trouble.

The name appears in Assyrian and, later, Persian inscriptions, in Talmudic texts, and, increasingly, in Greek and Latin writings. It also occurs in surviving inscriptions from the ancient southern Arabian civilization dating from the late pre-Christian and early Christian centuries. In these, the term denotes the nomadic as distinct from the sedentary population. The 'Arab' appears as a bedouin, sometimes as a raider. The first attested use of the name by Arabs of themselves, in Arabic, occurs in an early fourth century CE inscription announcing the death and the achievements of the leader of the nomads of northern and central Arabia, who describes himself as 'King of all the Arabs'. This inscription is also the earliest surviving record of the Arabic language.

The name Persia – in Hebrew *Pāras* – appears in two verses in Ezekiel (27:10 and 38:5), where it is listed, along with other remote places, to indicate the outer limits of the known world. The Persians make a more dramatic appearance in the writing on the wall at Belshazzar's feast, *mene mene tekel u-pharsin*, which being interpreted informed the unhappy Babylonian prince that he was weighed in the balances and found wanting, and that his kingdom would be divided and given to the Medes and Persians (Daniel 6:25–28). The post-exilic books of the Hebrew Bible often reflect this perception of the Persian conquests of the sixth century BCE as a fulfilment of God's purpose. This comes out most strongly in Isaiah (44:28 and 45:1), when the Persian king Cyrus is spoken of as God's shepherd and even as God's anointed (Hebrew *mashiah*).

The wars between the Persians and the Greeks, and later the Romans, earned the Persians an important place in classical historiography and literature. Until the modern decipherment of the ancient Persian inscriptions, the classics and the Bible supplied virtually all that was known about pre-Islamic Iran. Neither was read in Muslim Iran.

The name 'Turk' first occurs in Chinese and a little later in Byzantine writings. Chinese annals of the sixth century CE speak of the Tu Kiu, who founded a powerful empire stretching from the borders of China westward across Central Asia. The same people are named in Byzantine annals as the Tourkoi. In 568 CE, we are told, their chief, the Khagan, sent an ambassador to Constantinople seeking the emperor's support against the Persians. Thereafter, the various Central Asian Turkic tribes and empires are often mentioned by both their Far Eastern and Middle Eastern neighbours. The first use of the name Turks by Turks to describe themselves, in a recognizably Turkish language, occurs in a set of runic inscriptions discovered near the Orkhon River, in northern Mongolia. These inscriptions date from the eighth century CE, and contain the royal annals of a short-lived Turkish empire extending from the Chinese to the Persian frontiers. A little later we find Turkish writings of various kinds in Central Asia, in scripts mostly derived from Aramaic. These include both Christian and Buddhist writings, showing the extent to which the Turks had been exposed to both Middle Eastern and Asian religions. Their major historical role however was as Muslims, and in the lands of Islam.

They first entered the Middle East as slaves, captured by Arab and Persian raiders beyond the Islamic frontier in Central Asia, and were valued especially for their military qualities. They soon became a significant and in time a predominant element in the armies of the caliphs and sultans of Islam. Before long, the Turkish slave soldiers were led by Turkish officers and, in time, commanded by Turkish generals. For a while they were prized for their loyalty to the princes whom they served, but in a period of political fragmentation and anarchy, they began to play an independent role, first as condottieri, then as governors, finally as independent rulers.

For some time they remained a small alien minority in the Middle Eastern lands where they lived, among the peoples whom they ruled. This changed when Turkish tribes began to migrate from Central Asia into Iran and the nearer East. These came not as individual slaves or adventurers, but as free peoples who settled among the existing inhabitants and in some regions assimilated them to their own Turkish culture. In all the lands of the Middle East they established a domination which lasted for almost a thousand years. They left a string of Turkish nation-states extending from Central Asia to the Mediterranean, as well as significant Turkish-speaking populations under foreign rule.

The Arab attitude toward the Turks, as reflected in literature, went through several phases. On first contact, they were seen as primitive and uncouth, but with the virtues as well as the defects of the 'noble savage'. As they assumed a military role, they acquired new images; first as brave and honourable soldiers, then, as the soldiers became rulers, as harsh oppressors. But more generally in medieval times, the coming of the Turks to the Middle East was regarded more as a blessing than as a curse. In the words of the greatest of Arab historians, Ibn Khaldūn:

When the state was drowned in decadence ... it was God's benevolence that He rescued the faith by reviving its dying breath ... and defending the walls of Islam. He did this by sending to the Muslims, from the Turkish nation ... rulers to defend them and utterly loyal helpers ... Islam rejoices in the benefit which it gains through them, and the branches of the kingdom flourish with the freshness of youth.[2]

This view was not exceptional; nor was it unanimous. There was no lack of negative as well as positive images and stereotypes, but during the age when Islam was being attacked by Christian Crusaders from the west and heathen Mongols from the east, the Turks were seen as saviours of the faith. When both enemies disappeared – the Crusaders defeated and ejected, the Mongols Islamized and assimilated, the Arabic and Persian-speaking masses became more aware and more resentful of what, increasingly, some of them saw as a barbarian domination.

There were of course always rivalries and indeed at times hostilities between these different ethnic groups, and these are reflected in a whole literature of ethnic slurs and jokes in Arabic, Persian and Turkish. In modern times these antagonisms have been intensified and even systematized under the impact of new nationalist ideologies.

In traditional society, an ethnic difference distinguishing the ruling dynasty and elite from the mass of the population was seen as neither odd nor offensive, as long as all were united in the brotherhood of Islam. For most of the history of the Ottoman Empire, the Ottomans were accepted as the legitimate rulers of a great Muslim state, and membership of the ruling elite was open to all Ottoman subjects who professed Islam and could use the Turkish language. Exceptions even to these requirements were sometimes allowed. It was not until the late nineteenth century that the notion was implanted among the non-Turkish-speaking – primarily Arabic-speaking – Muslim inhabitants that this was a Turkish rather than a Muslim empire, and that they were therefore a subject people rather than an equal participant in the Ottoman polity.

Anti-Turkish feeling among Arabs on a serious scale first appeared in the last stages of the Ottoman Empire and was clearly due to foreign influences – on the one hand the new idea of nationalism and consequently of a greater Arab nation suppressed by alien Turkish domination; on the other, the direct incitement and intervention of outside powers. In time, these forces combined to bring about the overthrow of the Ottoman Empire and the dismemberment of its territories. In so doing, what they created was not a greater Arab nation, but a string of Arab states.

SIX

The State

People may define their identity by country, by nation, by culture, by religion, but the allegiance they owe is payable to the state, which collects taxes, raises armies, employs civil servants, enforces law and may also dispense some benefits. In a sense, this has always been so, since rulers first learned not just how to seize, but also how to delegate and transmit authority. The bureaucratic state is probably older in the Middle East than anywhere else in the world. In its various stages of development from antiquity to the present day, its strength has been reinforced by both water and oil – the one through the control of irrigation in river-valley societies, the other by the handling of money in economies dependent on oil-revenues. Modern technologies of transport and surveillance, of domination and repression, have further strengthened the power of the state over its subjects. At the present time, in the Middle East as in many other places, the state by which he is ruled, more than any other factor, determines a man's identity.

For most of the period since the advent of Islam, there have been only Islamic states in the Middle East. The Persian Empire was entirely conquered; the Byzantine Empire was pushed back, province by province, and finally extinguished with the Turkish conquest of Constantinople. The states founded by the Crusaders in the Levant lasted for a while, but were liquidated, and their territories reincorporated in the Islamic world.

In principle, there was only one universal Islamic state. Ideally, and for the while even in practice, the Islamic polity was a single State bound together by the faith and law of Islam and ruled by a single sovereign, the Caliph. The desire to realize this ideal remained a recurring theme and a powerful motive through the centuries of Islamic history. In fact, however, after the early centuries this was never so. There was not one state, but many states; not one ruler, but many rulers interacting in peace, commerce, diplomacy, and war.

Obviously, it was necessary somehow to regulate relations between them, to set up a kind of Muslim international law. In textbooks and treatises on the Holy Law of Islam, the discussion of international law, or of anything that in modern parlance might be called international law, appears to be concerned only with relations between the Muslim state – the one and only Muslim state – and non-Muslim states. But in fact of course there were many Muslim states, and Islamic law accommodated this in the way that it accommodated some other unpalatable realities, by means of what is called a 'legal device' (*hīla shar'iyya*). The device used for this purpose was the legal discussion of war conducted against bandits and rebels, recognized as legitimate forms of warfare. The law makes a clear distinction. Bandits are merely bandits, to be treated and punished as criminals. Rebels, on the other hand, are a recognized legal category, with belligerent rights and certain other rights, including even the levying of taxes and the administration of justice. From the way in which the principle of 'warfare against rebels' was applied, it is clear that what was involved was a kind of intra-Islamic international law, regulating relations between Muslim states. This conveniently left open the question of which was the legitimate ruler and which the rebel, each naturally considering himself the legitimate ruler and the other the rebel. This made dealings between Muslim states in peace and in war legally possible and agreements between them valid and enforceable.

One example may serve. The Treaty of Amasya, agreed in 1555 between the Shah of Persia and the Sultan of Turkey at the end of a long war, is commonly accepted by historians as one of the most important international treaties in the Middle East in that period. Yet if one looks through the archival or published Ottoman collections of treaties, the Treaty of Amasya is not there. These collections, until a very late date, preserve only treaties between the Ottoman Empire and Christian states. Christian states were a legal reality. Another Muslim state was not a legal reality. From the point of view of the Sultan, the Shah was a rebel; from the point of view of the Shah, the Sultan was a rebel, and they agreed to leave the question open. An Ottoman manual of the scribal art provides two relevant documents. The first, aptly headed 'A Letter of Supplication', purports to come from the Shah, but was obviously drafted by an Ottoman official. To this the Sultan graciously responds in what is presented as a unilateral statement from his side, but in fact incorporates the terms of the agreement. There was no doubt an equivalent document on the Persian side.

The Islamic world, now in its fifteenth century, embraces a billion people and a vast area in many continents. With the collapse of the last great universal Islamic empire, that of the Ottomans, in 1918, the dream of unity was for a while abandoned, and Muslims sought to adjust to changed circumstances. The problem was not entirely new. Since the days of the break-up of the original Caliphate, Muslim peoples had in fact, though not in theory, been divided into separate political entities, had created political institutions, and had organized themselves to take political action. How did they do so?

The answer to these questions may be found in certain habits and institutions, deeply rooted in the past and still very active at the present time. One of them is the State – not the nation, not the country but the State itself, the integrated, coercive power in the community, and the ganglion of interrelated, interacting careers and interests that controls it. Another is the army, on which the state depends for its survival.

The armies of Islam consisted traditionally of tribal levies and of slaves. The former were usually short-term volunteers; the latter, from the classical Mamluks to the Ottoman Janissaries, were alien. Both were therefore cut off from the mass of the urban and peasant population.

The introduction of the European practice of conscription in the early nineteenth century brought both peasants and townsfolk, for the first time, into close and continued relationship with the state and with those who exercised the state authority. Previously, their direct experience of the state authority had been limited to the collection of taxes and the enforcement of law. Both of these demanded obedience. Neither of them required or inspired any sentiment of loyalty. With conscription, the common man's experience of the state acquired a whole new dimension. Through conscription, ordinary people became for the first time part of the apparatus of the state, and, again for the first time, became involved with people and places outside their immediate village or neighbourhood. The need for officers, and more especially for corporals and sergeants, gave some the chance and many more the hope of participating in the exercise of state authority. Such new devices as uniforms and badges, flags and anthems, gave symbolic form to this new common identity.

The new army needed officers of a new kind; the new state needed vastly increased numbers of clerks. To provide these, the state for the first time involved itself in education, a service previously provided and directed by the men of religion and funded by the discretionary beneficence of princes and other persons of wealth. Graduates from the new schools and colleges for the most part entered the service of the state, military or civilian. This was the purpose for which they were created; this was the ambition of their alumni. For a while, even the graduates of the new medical schools tried to find jobs as civil servants; it was only the less successful who actually practised medicine.

All this brought a significant increase in literacy, which in turn helped and was helped by the emergence of the media. The first printing presses in the Middle East were Jewish and, later, Christian; the first newspapers in the region were products and instruments of the French Revolution, published by the French embassy in Istanbul and Bonaparte's administration in Egypt. Some other newspapers and periodicals followed, mostly due to European enterprise and Christian missions, and with a very limited readership and impact. In the course of the nineteenth century they were completely overshadowed by the new gazettes and newspapers published first in Egypt and Turkey and then all over the region. At first, these were state enterprises, established and conducted to accomplish state purposes. In a leading article, the official Ottoman monitor in 1832 explained that this publication was the natural successor of the long line of imperial historiographers and served the same purpose: 'to make known the true nature of events and the real purport of the acts and commands of the government', so as to prevent misunderstanding and to forestall uninformed criticism. Even when, later, privately owned media were established, they remained under state control or supervision. In most countries in the region they remain so at the present day.

The circulation of newspapers, and more generally communication between different parts of the region, received a great impetus when the Ottoman government established a national postal service in 1834. The advent of the telegraph in 1855 – thanks to the needs of the Crimean War – and the construction of the first railways in 1866 all helped to extend and consolidate the power of the state.

In the twentieth century, the newspaper and the printing

press were supplemented first by radio, then by television. Thanks to these, the control of the state over the minds and sentiments of its people was further reinforced – but with the growth of international broadcasting it was also, for the first time, seriously challenged. The communications revolution is sharpening that challenge.

Like armies and ministries, official newspapers and radio stations did not have, as their immediate purpose, to serve the country or the nation or the community. They served the state, by which they were often created, maintained, and usually controlled. The state, more often than not, meant the ruler and the small group of people helping him in the exercise of his autocratic power.

Dynasticism has been a powerful force in Middle Eastern history, and has often acquired even a religious connotation. The promised Messiah of the Jews was to be of the house of David; the *saoshyant* of Iran, of the sacred seed of Zoroaster. Muslims in general accord a special respect to the descendants of the Prophet; the Shī'a believe that the headship of the Islamic community belongs to these descendants by right, and that Muslim rulers not of such descent are usurpers or at best, in principle at least, temporary substitutes. The Sunnis in theory rejected the hereditary principle in the headship of the community, the caliphate, and laid down a rule of election. But in practice, the early elective caliphate ended in a succession of regicides and civil wars, and sovereignty became dynastic in virtually every Muslim state. Even in the self-styled revolutionary republics at the present time, such rulers as Saddam Hussein in Iraq and Hafiz al-Assad in Syria are grooming their sons to succeed them. Sometimes the dynastic name was extended to the state, the country, and even the nationality. The best known example from the past is the Ottoman Empire; from the present day, the Saudi monarchy. Both derive their names from the founder of the ruling house.

For many centuries now, and in most of the region until the present day, there have been only two ways of changing the government. One is succession within a ruling family;

the other is the removal and replacement of the ruler by the use or threat of force. Dynastic succession was until modern times the only generally accepted title to legitimacy. Those who acceded by force have usually tried to achieve the same kind of legitimacy for their own successors. Apart from the royal houses of Morocco and Jordan, both descended from the Prophet, most monarchies in the Arab world since the end of the Caliphate have been founded or taken over by rebellious governors, disloyal officers, impatient princes, or restless tribal chiefs. The modern age has added a remarkable new phenomenon – hereditary revolutionary leadership.

The great strength of monarchy in determining allegiance, and with it identity, is that it provides stability and continuity. More specifically, it offers a form of peaceful, recognized succession. The European dynastic rule of primogeniture was not normally followed in Muslim monarchies, where the more usual practice was for each incumbent to nominate a suitable heir from among the members of his family. The successor might be, and frequently was, a brother, a nephew, or even a cousin. Heredity and election remain the only accepted forms of legitimate succession lasting over long periods. Where they are corrupted or overthrown, only violence remains – the seizure of power by conspiracy, assassination, coup d'état, or armed insurrection. Election – known in theory but never actually practised – seemed to offer another way.

In modern democratic republics peaceful succession is ensured by elections held at prescribed intervals and under fixed rules. Electoral democracy in the Middle East has had a brief and chequered history. It flourished for a while in Lebanon but was ended by foreign invasion and internal dissension. It continues to function in Turkey and Israel, though in both it is subject to threats of different kinds. The Islamic Republic of Iran holds regular elections for both the presidency and parliament, and these are genuinely contested. But candidates for both must be scrutinized and approved by a committee of religious experts, and the elected President ranks third in the ruling hierarchy, after two unelected seniors with total executive control. With all these restrictions, the Iranian system probably allows more freedom of debate and dissent than most others in the region.

Egypt has evolved a unique system of its own – a kind of monarchical presidency combined with a quasi-parliamentary, quasi-electoral system. As the presidency has evolved since the Revolution of 1952–1954, each president chooses and appoints his successor, not, as was customary in the past, within a single royal, princely, or sheikhly family, but among the ruling group of officers. A few other states have experimented, cautiously, with elected bodies. Elsewhere, most of the region is divided between monarchies, tyrannies, and some regimes that combine features of both.

A remarkable feature of the modern age and of the changes which modernization has brought to Islam has been the strengthening, not the weakening of the State as a focus of activity. One reason for this is an important internal development. In the traditional Islamic society, the power of the State was in both theory and practice limited. There is a common tendency to think of Islamic political tradition as conducive to despotic, even capricious rule, and this view may appear to receive some support from recent events. It is, however, based on a misreading of Islamic history and law. The traditional Islamic State may have been autocratic; it was not despotic. The power of the sovereign was restricted by a number of factors, some legal, some social. It was limited in principle by the holy law which, being of divine origin, precedes and rules the State. The State and the sovereign, according to this principle, are subject to the law and are in a sense established and authorized by the law and not, as in some systems, the other way round.

In addition to this theoretical restraint, there were also practical restraints. In traditional Islamic societies, there were many well entrenched interests and intermediate powers which imposed effective limits on the ability of the State to control its subjects. These included, in all times and places, the military and religious establishments. Often, in the eighteenth and early nineteenth centuries, that is to say in the period immediately preceding modernization, they included both a rural aristocracy and an urban patriciate. With the process of modernization in the Islamic world, these intermediate powers have one by one been weakened or taken over, leaving the State with a far greater degree of autocratic control over its subjects than it ever enjoyed in traditional Islamic societies. And while on the one hand the limiting powers have dwindled or disappeared, the State itself now has at its disposal the whole modern apparatus of domination. The result is that present-day states in the Islamic world, even those claiming to be progressive and democratic, are – in their domestic affairs at least – vastly stronger than the so-called tyrannies of the past.

This may help us to understand another somewhat surprising phenomenon of the recent and current Middle Eastern world – the extraordinary persistence of states once created. Before the First World War, there were in effect only two – or we might say two-and-a-half or perhaps two-and-three quarters – states in the Middle East. The two were of course the surviving monarchies of Turkey and Iran. Both were conceived not as nation states in the modern Western sense, but as universal Muslim empires, and it was only in comparatively recent times that they began to adopt territorial and national designations in their protocol and official usage.

The half is Egypt. From the tenth century onwards, Egypt, previously a province in the empire of the Caliphs, became the seat of an independent Muslim power, often ruling over Syria, Palestine and western Arabia as well as the Nile Valley. The rulers and soldiers were usually from elsewhere – Berbers, Kurds, Turks, Circassians and others – but their administration, which ensured the survival and stability of the realm, was overwhelmingly Egyptian.

The Ottoman conquest of 1517 ended Egypt's independence; the British occupation in 1882 made it subject to a European imperial power. Yet, despite external suzerainty and foreign occupation, Egyptians retained a large measure of autonomy in their internal affairs. Under fairly remote Ottoman and then somewhat less remote British control, Egypt continued to function as a political entity, with a locally-based ruler, government and civil service in the Nile Valley, administering what in effect, if not in name, amounted to an Egyptian state. The modern state of Egypt, under the monarchy and then the Republic, is thus no recent creation, but the result of a long process of political evolution and experience.

Another state with a tradition of semi-independence and internal autonomy is Lebanon. Superficially, Lebanon would seem to be one of the numerous new states fashioned out of the debris of the Ottoman Empire at the end of the First World War. But Lebanon differed significantly from the others. It rested on an established living tradition of autonomy and a sense of separate identity maintained for centuries. This was not the so-called 'Greater Lebanon' devised by the French as a support for their rule; the 'Little Lebanon' consisted of the mountain, with a rough rectangle of territory running from just south of Tripoli to just north of Sidon, and extending inland. Its population was predominantly Christian, mostly Maronite, with minorities of Druze and Shī'a. This region had enjoyed a large measure of autonomy under local chieftains, which was generally respected by the Ottomans, and its people had built up a distinctive way of life. The Maronites, belonging to a Uniate church in communion with Rome, had long maintained contact with Christian Europe. From 1861 until the First World War, the Lebanon was governed by a special regime known as the *Règlement organique*, with an elective administrative council headed by a (non-Lebanese) Christian governor. After the collapse of the Ottoman Empire and the installing of the French Mandate, the new rulers did not restore the *Règlement organique*; instead they added a number of neighbouring districts to the original Lebanese territory. The intention was no doubt to strengthen the

Lebanese base by increasing its size; the effect in the long run was to divide and weaken it by increasing its population.

Another area of old-established self-independence was Arabia. Nominally under Ottoman suzerainty, the greater part of the peninsula was in fact left to its own devices, and was ruled by local dynasties, mostly of tribal origin. Like the states of the Fertile Crescent, they acquired their independence through the break-up of empires, but both the frontiers and the forms of their states were shaped by the play of Arabian, not of imperial politics.

The rest of the Middle East had had no experience of separate statehood or of the exercise of political sovereignty for a very long time. The nations who lived there had merged their identities in the larger communal and dynastic loyalties; the countries in which they lived were no more than imperial provinces; their very names and boundaries were subject to frequent change, and – with the exception of Egypt – had little historical significance or even geographical precision.

As a result of two world wars and of the extension and withdrawal of European imperial power, a whole series of new States was set up, with frontiers and even identities largely devised by colonial administration and imperial diplomacy. Their structures and their infrastructures were similarly provided. The 1930s and 1940s brought new models of government from Europe: the Party and the Leader. Political parties had appeared in several Middle Eastern countries during the brief intervals of parliamentary democracy introduced by revolutionary movements in Iran and Turkey and by foreign rulers in Egypt and the Fertile Crescent. The system of the single party as a central element in the apparatus of government – the Communist Party in the Soviet Union, the Fascist Party in Italy, the Nazi Party in Germany – was new. Germany and Italy were already seen as models of a successful struggle for national unification. Many looked to them now as models of how to achieve and then to exercise authority in the national state. This ideology reached its apogee in the Ba'th Party, founded in Vichy-controlled Syria in 1941 to organize support for the pro-Axis Rashid Ali regime in Iraq. Rival branches of the Ba'th Party rule both these countries at the present time and sustain their respective Leaders, Saddam Hussein and Hafiz al-Assad. Like their long-departed European predecessors in Leadership, each of these in his country is the very embodiment of the state, and loyalty to him is the ultimate definition of membership of the community.

The Soviet Communist Party long survived the German and Italian fascist models, and in the second half of the twentieth century, socialism, in one form or another, became the predominant ideology. While socialism did nothing to improve the economy, it enormously strengthened the power of the state over its subjects.

One of the most extraordinary features of the modern Middle East is indeed this strength of the states and their ability to resist pressures either to disintegrate into their local components or to coalesce into some larger union. Some of these new States rested on genuine historical entities; some were entirely artificial. Nevertheless, in spite of the very strong ideological urge towards unification arising from pan-Arabism, with one exception, none of these Arab states has disappeared. However artificial and unnatural they may appear, however alien in their origins, however ancient the cultures on which they are superimposed, the states, even the most improbable of them, have shown a remarkable capacity for self-preservation and survival, often in very adverse circumstances. There have been many attempts to unite or at least to associate two or more Arab states. No such attempt has so far lasted for very long. Even the reunion of North and South Yemen – historically one country, divided by the British occupation of Aden – is obviously proving extremely difficult. In earlier days, failure in attempts at Arab unity could be – and of course was – attributed to outside influence. The record of more recent attempts illustrates that whatever the role of outside influence in the past, it is no longer an adequate explanation at the present. The barriers to greater Arab unity arise inside and not outside the Arab world, and the failure of the mergers testifies to the remarkable persistence and the growing power of the state itself as a political factor.

Perhaps the most dramatic illustration of the effectiveness of state loyalty was the failure of both Iraq and Iran to subvert their enemies during the first Gulf war. The Arabs of Iran, like the Shī'a of Iraq, resisted appeals to national or sectarian sentiments, and remained loyal to their country and its government.

A more negative example of the primacy of statehood in the definition of identity and allegiance is provided by the fate of the Palestinian refugees in 1948 and after. In Jordan – the other half of the former Palestine Mandate – the Nationalities Law of 1954 conferred Jordanian citizenship on all who held Palestinian citizenship before the end of the Mandate and resided in the Jordanian kingdom thereafter 'except Jews'. In other Arab states where the Palestinians found refuge, they and their locally born descendants remain, to the third generation, refugees, that is to say, stateless aliens. The late P.J. Vatikiotis once remarked that the core of the Palestinian problem in its later phase was not so much a people in search of a country, as a political elite in search of a state. The resettlement in 1947 of many millions of refugees in India and Pakistan; the absorption, a few years earlier, of millions of displaced Germans and Poles into West Germany and Poland, reflect different perceptions of the relative significance of peoplehood, nationhood and statehood, resulting from the historical experiences of the Indian subcontinent and of central and eastern Europe. The involvement of the United Nations in the Palestine case, and not in the others, may also have contributed to the difference.

One reason for the strength of the state is the opportunities which it provides for those who control it. Each of these states has, in the course of the years, evolved a new governing elite of whom Adolphus Slade, one of the most acute Western observers of the evolving Middle East of his day, remarked: 'The State is the estate of the new nobility.'[3]

Another still more compelling reason, effective even with those who derive little benefit from the state, is the fear of what may happen when the state disintegrates into its component parts. This happened during the civil war in Lebanon; it threatened in Iraq in the aftermath of the Gulf War. There are other countries where this menacing possibility is clearly visible. The horrors of the Lebanese civil war – a situation where, in the bitter Lebanese joke of the time, even the law of the jungle was not respected – is sufficiently well-known to act as a terrible warning. In countries like Iraq, where a major part of the national revenue derives from a single source, oil royalties, and where the resulting wealth is controlled and dispensed by the government, such fragmentation is less likely. The centralizing power of money is buttressed by the superior armed force which that money buys for the central government. In unstable countries which do not or no longer enjoy that advantage, fragmentation and civil war are an ever-present danger.

SEVEN

Symbols

The modern world is full of symbols of identity, both visual and auditory. Nations have flags and anthems, and the members of the international community are represented, in a variety of contexts, by a whole menagerie of birds and beasts, most of them fierce and dangerous, like lions, eagles, dragons and bears, or at least truculent, like the cock. There are also plants which fulfil a similar purpose, such as the rose, the shamrock, the thistle and the maple-leaf. Emblems may also express doctrinal and ecclesiastical differences, like the schism between the Eastern and Western churches. Adherence to one or the other is symbolized by the display of the different shapes of the Greek and Latin crosses. In the Western world, and now also elsewhere, a host of voluntary associations – colleges, societies, political parties, corporations, unions, sports clubs – have their distinguishing emblems, badges or even caps, shirts and ties, by which members identify themselves to one another.

In the West, this symbolic language of identity and

recognition springs from old roots, and is the result of a long evolution. In the modern Middle East, much of it is new, sometimes imposed, mostly copied from outside. The introduction of national anthems and the brass bands that play them dates from the early nineteenth century, when the reforming Ottoman Sultan Mahmūd II, in the course of modernizing his armed forces, requested the Sardinian ambassador in Istanbul to provide him with a bandmaster. The person chosen was Giuseppe Donizetti, a brother of the more famous Gaetano. Several Western visitors attest his success in forming and commanding what was officially designated as the 'Ottoman Imperial Music'. By now every sovereign state in the Middle East, as elsewhere, has a national anthem.

Another Western importation was the national flag, which symbolizes the national identity in design and colour, as the anthem does in blasts and drumbeats. Coats of arms of a sort were known in earlier times. In medieval Egypt and Syria, the sultans and the great amirs often had a kind of emblem or insignia, known in Arabic as *rank*, probably from the Persian *rang*, which simply means colour. These emblems were used in various ways – struck on coins, carved on buildings, and woven, engraved, or otherwise displayed on textiles, metalwork, and other objects. But they are rarely mentioned in historical writings, and seem to have had no political nor even much heraldic significance. The use of pennants and of battle flags in the Islamic Middle East is attested since very early times. These usually consisted of a piece of cloth of a single colour. Sometimes they represented an individual ruler or, more often, a dynasty. Thus, traditionally, the flag of the Umayyads was white, that of the Abbasids black, that of the House of the Prophet green. These three colours, representing the three major Arab dynasties, are combined in various ways in the flags of many present-day Arab states.

Today, every state in the Middle East, including patriarchal sheikhdoms, has a national flag. Most of these, like the flags of Western nations, consist of selected colours arranged in rectangles and triangles, and national flags and colours have an increasingly important part in a wide range of public events. A very popular Middle Eastern usage in the symbolism and imagery of emblems is the ceremonial, one might almost say incantatory, trampling and burning of the flags of most disfavoured nations.

Some, again like Western flags, make use of what are perceived as distinctive and identifying emblems. At first sight, these appear to be overwhelmingly religious. The flag of Israel includes the six-pointed star, known to Jews as the shield of David, long recognized as a Jewish emblem before it was incorporated in the flag of the newly-created State of Israel. The Saudi Arabian flag, with its stark juxtaposition of an unsheathed sword and the Muslim creed, vividly symbolizes one interpretation of Islam. The Turks, followed by some but not all other Muslim countries, incorporate the crescent, now generally seen as the emblem of Islam. Some have seen this use of the crescent as an affirmation of the centrality of Islam in their identity; others, as meaning no more than the use of the cross, and various derivatives from it, in the flags of such unfanatical Christian nations as the British and the Scandinavians. In the same way, the shield of David on the flag of Israel may be religious for some citizens; for others, it represents not so much religion as Jewish peoplehood, resurgent after the long use of this emblem by the Nazis, their precursors, and their imitators as a stigma of inferiority.

All these usages and their various interpretations are based on the assumption that the crescent and the shield of David are the emblems of the Muslim and Jewish faiths, having the same significance for Muslims and Jews as does the cross for Christians. This assumption has no basis either in history or in theology. For the Christian, the cross is a very powerful evocation, symbolizing the very core of his religious identity – the central dogma of his faith, the central event of his history. Neither the crescent nor the shield of David, has, or has ever had, any such significance. Both were simply used in decoration; both were used by people of different religions. The six-pointed star appears quite frequently as a decorative motif in Muslim architecture, as far west as Morocco, as far east as Pakistan. The crescent, sometimes with a six-pointed (or five-pointed or seven-pointed) star is attested in pre-Islamic Iran, as well as in Roman and Byzantine remains. Both crescent and star sometimes occur in Muslim religious contexts, along with other motifs, but had no special religious significance.

The, so to speak, sacralization of these two emblems was due to Christians, indulging in the common human error of attributing their own ideas and habits to others. For a long time, Christians referred to Muslims as Muhammadans, in the mistaken belief that Muhammad is for Muslims what Christ is for Christians. By a similar false analogy, they ascribed to the crescent and the shield of David a place equivalent to that of the cross among themselves. Muslims never did accept or use the term Muhammadan, which for them would be both inaccurate and blasphemous. They did however accept the crescent.

This process dates back to at least the sixteenth century. In paintings of the great Christian naval victory over the Turks at Lepanto in 1571, the Christian ships fly the cross; the Muslims ships fly the crescent. This emblem appeared quite frequently in Muslim decoration, no doubt including ships, and it was a natural error to assume that it was an Islamic emblem. But it was an error nonetheless. The clearest indication that in the sixteenth century the crescent was still just a decorative motif and not a religious emblem is a pair of trousers adorned with crescents, preserved in the Topkapı Palace Museum in Istanbul and formerly worn by Sultan Süleyman the Magnificent. This is surely a highly improbable use of a sacred religious emblem.

But in time, in a world dominated by Western, and therefore in some measure Christian, attitudes, both Muslims and Jews accepted and adopted the religious emblems that had been assigned to them, and by the present day they are universally recognized by followers of both religions.

While flags and emblems of state and church are alien to

Middle Eastern tradition, the practice of indicating identity, for both self-assertion and mutual recognition, by distinctive dress, is very old indeed in the region, and survives to the present day. Sometimes a sartorial mark of identity was imposed from above, to indicate – in a clear and immediately recognizable form – the difference between the rulers and the ruled. But it would seem from the historical record that such instructions were more often disregarded than enforced. In general, the assertion of identity through attire arose from internal need rather than external pressure. Peasants and herdsmen, members of feuding tribes, Jews and pagans, Christians and Muslims, as well as many others, proudly asserted their different identities by their dress, their footware, and most especially, their headgear.

This was seen as a social, at times a religious obligation. Already in the seventh century BCE a prophet warns the Jews of the punishment that God will inflict on 'all such as are clothed with strange apparel' (Zephaniah 1:8). Later, both rabbinic and Islamic authorities repeated injunctions to the faithful to maintain a clear difference between themselves and others in dress as well as in beliefs and practices. A man's headgear was especially important as indicating his religion, his affiliation, and sometimes also his social and occupational status. By Ottoman times it had become the practice to carve on the tombstone over a grave a representation of the distinctive headdress that the occupant had worn during his lifetime. One may thus easily identify the tomb of a Qadi, a Janissary officer, a civil servant at the Sublime Porte, and the like.

The beginnings of Westernization in the early nineteenth century gave a new declaratory importance to dress. Soldiers in the new Western-style army wore Western-style tunics, slacks and boots, and even their horses now wore Western instead of traditional harness and accoutrements. Only the headgear remained as the last bastion of the old order. The turban had indeed long since acquired a special significance. A tradition ascribed to the Prophet defines the turban as the barrier between belief and unbelief. More commonly, it was used to mark the distinction between the professional men of religion and the rest of the community. In Turkey, with the reforms of Kemal Atatürk, even this last bastion fell to reform, and the turbans, fezzes and other traditional headgear were replaced by a variety of European-style hats and caps.

For some of the present-day movements of religious revival, both Muslim and Jewish, a return to traditional clothes and accessories has acquired a similar symbolic meaning. One small example is the adoption of Hasidic costume by newly devout Jews in Israel – those who, in the accepted phrase, 'return in repentance'. Another is the new significance of the necktie, avoided by pious Muslims who otherwise wear Western coats, shirts, and trousers. In a curious counterpart of the earlier Christian sacralization of the crescent, the necktie – perhaps because of its vaguely cruciform shape – has become, for some Muslims, a Christian emblem and therefore a mark of obeisance to Western hegemony.

For women, the revolution in dress was more dramatic and also more dangerous. In some parts of the Islamic world, notably in Iran and Afghanistan, it remains so to the present day. Two garments have acquired a special symbolic importance: the veil, hiding the face, and the scarf, hiding the hair. For women in the East, they are emblems; for the pious, of submission, for the emancipated, of repression. For Muslim women in the West they have sometimes become the blazons of a proud assertion of identity.

EIGHT

Aliens and Infidels

An essential part of any definition of identity is the line that divides Self from Other, Insider from Outsider. Different definitions of identity will require different lines, and these lines may at various times shift, overlap, and intersect. But wherever they may be drawn there is always, at least in people's minds, a clear division between 'us' and 'them'. The definition of the Other is an essential part of the definition of the Self.

In our modern world, the one universally accepted criterion of political definition and differentiation is that provided by the nation-state. All men and women are divided into citizens and aliens, and the distinction between them is defined by law, applied in practice, and accepted as legitimate. There are some further distinctions between citizens, and for that matter among aliens, which also exist and may sometimes be effective. But these other distinctions are, so to speak, furtive and socially disapproved. In civilized countries at least, they lack legal sanction.

The legal barrier between citizen and alien is permeable, and can be crossed by a process known nowadays as naturalization. In this it differs significantly from the more primitive but still widely applied criteria of kinship, ethnicity, and race, but resembles the distinction by religion which also – for some though not for all religions – can be crossed by the process of conversion.

At the present day and indeed for some time past, the Middle East and more generally the Islamic world has, at least legally and formally, accepted the modern Western pattern of identity and difference by citizenship. The Islamic world today is divided into a number of nations, in most of which native non-Muslims are citizens but Muslim non-citizens are aliens. There are also large and growing numbers of Muslims living as minorities in countries with non-Muslim majorities in Asia and Africa, and latterly also in Europe and the Americas. For these minorities, especially in the democratic West, the question of relations between Muslims and others arises in a new and largely unprecedented form.

But the older sense of religious identity was not effaced. Indeed it survived, much more strongly than in Europe, first because the change was much more recent, and second because the original predominance of religious identity and allegiance was far more profound. In recent years we have seen a reassertion of Islamic principles and attitudes, primarily of course by the rulers of revolutionary Iran, but also by important and influential groups of people in other lands. This resurgence of Islam also implies, within itself, a reassertion of classical Islamic perceptions of the place of religion in determining social and political identity, a reassertion, that is, of Islam as the primary definition of identity and source of legitimacy for Muslims. More and more we find that in Muslim countries, not only in Iran, it is Islamic standards, arguments and vocabulary that are being used either to defend or to challenge a government, either to justify the legitimacy of an existing regime, or to formulate a critique of that regime and offer an alternative to it. For many, Islam has again become the primary criterion of distinction between brother and stranger. In the age of nationality and nationalism, an Iraqi or Egyptian Muslim sees an Iraqi or Egyptian Christian as a compatriot, sharing the same homeland and the same long and glorious history. In the perspective of Islam, his Christian compatriots and his heathen ancestors are both alien to him, and the only true identity and therefore the only true brotherhood is that of the community of believers.

This idea is, of course, not new. It is fundamental in classical Islamic legal and political doctrine, and has often been reasserted in the twentieth century against what are seen as the disruptive heresies of the nationalists. In 1917 the grand vizier of the Ottoman Empire, Said Halim Pasha, declared flatly, 'The fatherland of a Muslim is wherever the Sharī'a prevails.'[4] The same idea was set forth more recently by the late Ayatollah Khomeini in his oft-quoted dictum that 'There are no frontiers in Islam.' In other words, Islamic identity and loyalty pre-empt those of the country, the nation, or the nation-state.

But even among the most extreme exponents of these views, they have not always been strictly applied. There were, for example, some small islands, the Tumbs and Abū Mūsā, at the southern end of the Persian Gulf, which had been Arabian but which had been seized and occupied by the late Shah of Iran. After the Iranian revolution the previous owners suggested politely that the Islamic Republic might return these islands. They have not yet been returned, nor is there any indication that they are likely to be. Another example: the constitution of the Islamic Republic of Iran, which in general is religious rather than national or patriotic in its terminology, nevertheless lays down that the President of the Republic must be Iranian by birth and origin. This is more than is required by the Constitution of the United States, where it is sufficient to be born in the United States to be eligible for the presidency. That this restriction in Iran is not just theoretical was demonstrated some years ago, when a candidate for the presidency was disqualified because, though of Iranian birth, he was of Afghan parentage.

In examining Muslim perceptions of the Other, it may be useful to compare Islamic attitudes and perceptions with those of the two kindred Middle Eastern religions. Judaism, Christianity and Islam are three religions that are historically connected, geographically adjacent, theologically akin. Compared with the other great religions of the world, the differences between them seem insignificant, the resemblances overwhelming. For most of their history, all three religions have been far more aware of each other than of the remoter faiths of the world. Each has been acutely conscious of the challenges offered by the others, and relations between them have been embittered, not only by their differences but also – perhaps more especially – by their resemblances.

Nowadays, it has become the custom in the West to speak of 'the Judaeo-Christian tradition' and sometimes to contrast it with what is perceived as a different Islamic tradition. The term is new, and in earlier times would probably have been found equally offensive on both sides of the hyphen. But it designates a genuine historical and cultural phenomenon. Christianity retained the Jewish Bible and, re-naming it the Old Testament, added a New Testament to it. Islam dropped both. One need only think of the immense significance of the Old Testament in Christian literature, music and art to see the importance of this shared Judaeo-Christian element.

But one could, with equal validity – referring to the past if not to the present – speak of a Judaeo-Islamic tradition or even of an Islamo-Christian tradition. Judaism and Islam are both legal religions, believing in a divinely ordained law which regulates every aspect of life – public and private, civil and criminal, domestic and public, ritual and dietary, by the same authority and with the same sanctions. The Christian dichotomy between God and Caesar, church and state, imperium and sacerdotium, is alien both to the Judaic and the Islamic traditions. There is also a Judaeo-Muslim theological affinity. Jews and Muslims agree on a rigorous and uncompromising monotheism and reject basic Christian doctrines which they see as conflicting with that belief.

There are other criteria which would place Islam and Christianity together on one side and Judaism alone on the other. Judaism categorically rejects polytheism and idolatry, but otherwise makes no claim to exclusive truth. Monotheists of all peoples and persuasions, according to Rabbinic teaching, have a share in the world to come. For the Rabbis, Judaism is for Jews and those who care to join them; nobody is under any obligation to do so. Judaism claims that its truths are universal but not exclusive, and in this respect it seems closer to the religions of Asia than to either Islam or Christianity. Christianity and Islam both agreed that there is only one final revelation of God's truth and that salvation can only be achieved by that truth, preferably from its authorized exponents. Christian and Muslim alike shared this triumphalism, each convinced that his faith was the one true, whole and final religion, and that his cause would inevitably triumph. Muslims, like Christians, knew that those who did not share their beliefs would burn in everlasting hellfire. Unlike Christians, they saw no need to anticipate the divine judgment in this world.

Both possessors of God's last word believed they had a duty to bring this word to all humanity, that is, to convert the infidels, and to create an *oecumene* of their own in the process. The two religions contested the same Mediterranean world as the first step toward ultimate supremacy. This led to the long struggle of *jihād* and crusade, conquest and reconquest, through the centuries – the three major Muslim attacks on Europe: the Saracens in Sicily and Spain; the Turks in the Balkan peninsula; the Tatars in Russia; and of course the great European counter-attack which began with the reconquest of the homelands and went on to establish European Christian empires in most of the lands of Islam in more modern times.

In the course of the long struggle between these conflicting claims, both Christians and Muslims formed empires;

both came to rule over people of faiths other than their own, and confronted the problem of how to deal with such subjects. Until recently, the Jews faced no such dilemma. For virtually the whole period of Christian and Muslim history, the Jews were themselves subject people and Judaism was a minority religion, with no living tradition of how to rule over others. The modern state of Israel, though not constitutionally secular, aspires to the standard of the liberal democracies in this respect and still confronts the problem of combining a religious identity with a pluralistic modern polity.

The attitudes of the three to one another have also been profoundly affected by the historical sequence in which they appeared. For the Muslims, Judaism and Christianity were authentic revelations in their time but were outdated and superseded by the final and perfect revelation which is Islam. Muslim teachings also accuse the Christians and the Jews of having failed in their custodianship and having allowed the revelations entrusted to them to be corrupted and distorted. However, as precursor religions with originally authentic revelation, they are allowed to practise their religions and maintain their places of worship under Muslim authority, subject to the acceptance of certain discriminatory regulations. With some rare and atypical exceptions, this rule of tolerance has generally been observed by Muslim governments.

Islam, in the Christian perspective, was a different and far more dangerous adversary. Unlike Judaism, it was subsequent, not previous, and therefore necessarily false. Islam takes the same view of such post-Islamic religions as Babism and Bahaism. Unlike Judaism again, Islam and Christianity each represented a major political, military, and, for a while, intellectual threat to the other. Judaism in western Europe, despite persecutions and expulsions, survived. Islam, after the reconquest, was extirpated. The news from Europe suggests that even today, some Christians – and post-Christians – have difficulty in tolerating a Muslim presence in their midst.

During eight centuries of Muslim rule in Spain both Judaism and Christianity survived and in some limited measure flourished. The completion of the Christian reconquest in 1492 was followed within months by the expulsion of the Jews and within a few years by the expulsion of the Muslims from the peninsula. The restored identity of reconquered Christian Spain could not accept any Jewish or Muslim presence. The Muslim states, both in old and in newly conquered Muslim realms, were more tolerant. Except in Arabia, the Muslim holy land, they allowed non-Muslims to live under their rule and to share their countries, though not their identity. Indeed, until the impact of modern nationalist ideas, the question of such a sharing did not arise on either side.

The whole question of tolerance and intolerance – of the perception and acceptance of the religiously-defined other – is still very much distorted, among both Christians and Muslims, by polemic and mythology. Muslims denounce Christians for the aggressive fanaticism of the Crusades, forgetting that the Crusade itself was a long-delayed and limited response to the *jihād* and an attempt to win back by holy war what had been lost to a holy war. Christians accuse Muslims of bigotry, and forget that for many centuries Muslim lands provided a haven of refuge for victims of Christian persecution – not only Jews but also schismatic and heretical Christians.

Until very recently, there was no equivalent movement of migrants from Muslim to Christian lands – and the recent movement has other origins and raises other questions for both hosts and guests.

There are two other important differences between Islam and the other two religions. The first is that Islam, from its inception, perceives religion as a category, as a class of phenomena, and uses the word *dīn*, religion, as a noun with a plural. In the Qur'ān itself there is a famous and oft-cited verse: 'I have my religion, and you have your religion' (109:6), a notion which would surely have been very strange to Christians in earlier times. Another verse in the Qur'ān runs: 'There is no compulsion in religion' (2:256). A modern German scholar has interpreted this as an expression of resignation rather than of tolerance,[5] but the Muslim tradition has usually taken it as enjoining tolerance and forbidding the use of force, except in certain well-defined circumstances.

Islam, from the beginning, recognized that it had predecessors, and that some, having survived the advent of Islam, were also contemporaries. This meant that in Muslim scripture and in the oldest traditional theological and legal texts, certain principles were laid down, certain rules were established, on the treatment of those who follow other religions. This pluralism is part of the holy law of Islam, and these rules are on many points detailed and specific. Unlike Judaism and Christianity, Islam squarely confronts the problem of religious tolerance, and lays down both the extent and the limits of the tolerance to be accorded to the other faiths. For Muslims, the treatment of the religious other is not a matter of opinion or choice, of changing interpretations and judgments according to circumstances. It rests on scriptural and legal texts, that is to say, for Muslims, on holy writ and sacred law.

These texts and laws make certain basic distinctions among non-Muslim religions and their followers. The first and most crucial is theological. Certain specified religions possess a scripture which Islam recognizes as authentic, or rather, to be precise, as having been authentic. Three are named in the Qur'ān, as the Jews, the Christians, and the somewhat mysterious Sabians. In the Muslim perception, Judaism and Christianity were predecessors of Islam, earlier stages in the sequence of prophetic revelations sent by God to mankind, and thus in a sense of Islam itself. The Muslim list of prophets includes Adam, Noah, Abraham, Ishmael, Isaac, Jacob, Joseph, Lot, Moses, Aaron, David, Solomon, Jesus, John the Baptist, and other biblical figures. The scriptures given to the Jews and Christians are identified in the Qur'ān as the *Tawrāt*, that is the Pentateuch, brought by the prophet Moses; the Psalms brought by the prophet

David; and the Gospels brought by the prophet Jesus. All these were superseded and rendered unnecessary by the final and perfect revelation brought by the prophet Muhammad and contained in the Qur'ān. Since the followers of these earlier religions were chosen by God to receive authentic scriptures, still practise monotheism, and respect a holy text and a holy law, they are, despite their subsequent errors, to be accorded a certain measure of tolerance within the Muslim state, that is to say under a Muslim government.

That tolerance is defined and limited by law. It subjects its beneficiaries to discriminatory social and fiscal regulations, but in return it guarantees them the free exercise of their religions and, more than that, a very large measure of autonomy in the conduct of their internal affairs. They are to have full control of such matters as marriage, divorce, inheritance, and education, and, even more remarkably, have the power to maintain and enforce their decisions, if necessary calling upon the services of the public authorities. Since they are not Muslims, they are not bound to observe rules binding on Muslims but not on others. Islam forbids the drinking of alcohol, but Christians and Jews are, according to the traditional interpretation and application of the law, free to make, sell, and consume it. In classical Arabic literature, the Christian convent figures prominently in drinking songs and the like, since it was there that the poets and their friends would go when they wanted a drink. The word *der*, convent or monastery, acquired almost the sense of a tavern. In Ottoman times there are frequent orders to and by *qadis* trying to deal with the problem presented by Muslim guests at Jewish and Christian weddings, where wine flowed freely.

There is a rather charming story of a dervish who was imprisoned in Ottoman times for eating during the fasting month of Ramadan. That was of course a criminal offence, and he was therefore thrown into jail. Dervishes were notorious for being somewhat lax in their ritual observances. The story goes that the dervish looked out from between the bars in his cell, and saw a man in the street outside eating a kebab. And he called out to this man and said, 'Hey, you, it's Ramadan. If anyone sees you eating, they'll throw you into jail with me'. The man said, 'No, that's all right. I'm a Christian'. The dervish said in astonishment, 'Do you mean that because you're a Christian you're allowed to eat kebab in the street?' And he said, 'Yes, Ramadan doesn't apply to us'. To which the dervish said, 'You should give thanks to Allah every day that you are not of the true faith'.

Some modern Islamic governments have abandoned the old tolerance, and are enforcing Muslim religious law, including its penal provisions, on all their subjects irrespective of religion.

Those who follow a religion which is not specified as lawful, that is to say who do not have a recognized sacred scripture, are not to be allowed the tolerance of the Muslim state. Their choice is conversion or death, which may be commuted to enslavement. This did not present any great problem in the countries of the Middle East in the earliest areas of Islamic expansion – in the fertile crescent, North Africa, Sicily, Spain – because everybody was either Christian or Jewish. It presented some problems in Iran, where most people were Zoroastrians, and even more when the Muslims got to India and confronted Hindus, who were manifestly polytheist and appeared to be idol-worshippers. Eventually, legal formulas were found to accommodate all of these.

Those who, according to Sharī'a rules, qualified for tolerance were admitted to the *dhimma*, a pact between the Muslim state and a non-Muslim community, by which the state conceded certain privileges and the community accepted certain duties and constraints. A member of a community in possession of a *dhimma* was called a *dhimmī*. These constraints involved some limitations on the clothes the *dhimmīs* might wear, the beasts they might ride, the arms they might bear. There were limits on the building and use of places of worship. They were never to overtop mosques. No new ones were to be built, but old ones could be restored. Christians and Jews were to wear distinguishing garments, or emblems on their clothes. This was the origin of the *ghiyār*, the yellow patch which was first introduced by a caliph in Baghdad in the ninth century, and spread into Europe – for Jews – in later medieval times. *Dhimmīs* were required to avoid noise and display in their worship and ceremonies. Christians, for example, were to use clappers, not bells, in their churches. They were expected at all times to show respect for Islam and deference to Muslims. Most of these disabilities were social and symbolic rather than tangible and practical, and the evidence indicates that they were unevenly and intermittently applied. In the central lands at least, many of the social restrictions were more often disregarded than enforced. The one burden that was consistently imposed on the *dhimmīs* was the *jizya*, a poll-tax collected annually from every able-bodied adult male. This was maintained in all Islamic lands in all periods until the nineteenth century.

The rule of the *dhimma* led to another important difference in the status of religious minorities in Christendom and in Islam. In the Christian world, the behaviour of non-Christian minorities had only minimal and occasional effect on how they were treated. More commonly, the choice between tolerance and intolerance was decided in accordance with the inner logic of the dominant community, and there was little that the minorities themselves could do to influence the choice one way or the other. In Islam, the rules of the *dhimma* were familiar and well-understood and the *dhimmīs* knew perfectly well what behaviour would earn tolerance, what misbehaviour would provoke reprisals. The effects of this knowledge are very clear in the history and patterns of behaviour of the *dhimmī* communities and sometimes of their formally emancipated descendants.

The other classification of non-Muslims is political and military – into those who have been subjugated and those who have not yet been subjugated. The world is divided into the House of Islam and the House of War, the *Dār al-Islām* and the *Dār al-harb*. The *Dār al-Islām* is all those lands in which a Muslim government rules and the Holy Law of Islam prevails. Non-Muslims may live there on Muslim sufferance. The outside world, which has not yet been subjugated, is called the 'house of war', and strictly speaking a perpetual state of *jihād*, of holy war, is imposed by the law. The law also provided that the *jihād* might be interrupted by truces as and when appropriate. In fact, the periods of peace and war were not vastly different from those which existed between the Christian states of Europe for most of European history.

The law thus divides unbelievers theologically into those who have a book and profess what Islam recognizes as a divine religion and those who do not; politically into *dhimmīs*, those who have accepted the supremacy of the Muslim state and the primacy of the Muslims, and *harbīs*, the denizens of the *dār al-harb*, the house of war, who remain outside the Islamic frontier, and with whom therefore there is, in principle, a canonically obligatory perpetual state of war until the whole world is either converted or subjugated.

In time, an intermediate status, that of the temporary visitor, developed between the external alien and presumed enemy on the one hand, and the tolerated internal unbeliever. Non-permanent foreign residents could benefit from an agreement between the Muslim state and their own government. Such an agreement was called *amān*, and those who benefited from it were called *musta'min*. But 'temporary' could become a period of long duration, and quasi-permanent arrangements of this kind were approved for individuals and even for states. By the time of the Crusades, there were colonies of European Christian merchants in Muslim seaports, organized in communities under their own consular officials, and enjoying the privileges of the *dhimmī* communities without the fiscal and social disadvantages. Later, with the change in the power relationship between Christendom and Islam, these exemptions, originally freely granted by the Muslim state in accordance with the logic of its own institutions, became a system of extra-territorial privilege and immunity, imposed by force from one side and bitterly resented on the other.

A religious definition of group identity inevitably raises

the question of another kind of otherness, crucial in the history of Christendom; that of some intermediate status between the believer and the unbeliever – the schismatic, the heretic, the deviant.

Islamic experience, both past and present, shows many groups of deviants, who differed from mainstream Islam in belief or practice or both. There is a very rich polemic literature directed against such groups, far more extensive and more sophisticated than any polemics against non-Muslims. Deviance was serious; it was dangerous. It represented a real adversary. Such polemics occur mainly between the Sunnis and the Shī'a, the two major divisions of Islam. They also occur within each of these, between different schools or tendencies. Beginning in very early times, they continue to the present day.

Despite these divisions, there is no true equivalent of schism or heresy in Islam, in the Christian sense of these terms. In modern Arabic the word for heresy is *hartaqa*. Heresy and heretic in modern Arabic are loanwords, and it seems obvious, given the enormous number of deviant groups in Islam, that if Muslims had had a concept of heresy, they would have had a word for it. There are many names for many heresies, but no name for heresy.

Why? Again, one can see several reasons. Schism means split. There is no split in the sense of the schism between the Greek and Roman churches, because there is no institutional authority, and therefore no question of obedience or refusal. Heresy means choice and therefore, human nature being what it is, it is specialized to mean wrong choice. This again does not arise in Islam because there is considerable freedom of choice in matters of belief for Muslims, within very widely-drawn limits.

Despite frequent deviance and occasional repression, we find few of the legal, theological or practical implications of heresy which are found in Christendom. These were hardly possible in the absence of an institutional structure of authorities empowered to define and defend correct belief, to detect, correct, and where necessary punish error. All this, so characteristic of some Christian churches, had no real equivalent in Islamic history.

There were some exceptions. In the second half of the eighth century, the caliphs of Baghdad established a kind of inquisition and conducted an unmistakable persecution of Manichaeism, in the course of which many dissidents, not all of them Manichees, were detected, condemned and put to death. A little late, the Caliph al-Ma'mūn (813–833 CE) attempted to impose and enforce an officially-defined theological doctrine. It did not last long. In later medieval and early modern times, there were occasional persecutions of Sunnis in Shī'a countries, of Shī'a in Sunni countries and of Sufis in both. From time to time, there were even attempts at the forced conversion of non-Muslims, usually by a newly installed regime of militant reformers. But, broadly speaking, the use of force, against deviants as against *dhimmīs*, was rare, atypical, and due to special circumstances.

There are other reasons for this difference. Islam is not so much a matter of orthodoxy as of orthopraxy. It is what you do, not what you believe, that matters. Only God, it was argued, can judge sincerity in belief. What you do is a social fact and of concern to constituted authority. What Islam has generally asked of its believers is not textual accuracy in belief, but loyalty to the community and its constituted leader. This has led to a broad tolerance of deviation, until the point when it becomes disloyalty, easily equated with treason, or when it becomes seditious and subversive, a danger to the existing social and political order. When that happens, before very long the deviant crosses a boundary – not between orthodoxy and heterodoxy, which is relatively unimportant, but between Islam and apostasy. When deviation in belief reaches that point, it becomes an issue of law, a matter for action. And apostasy, according to all schools of Muslim jurisprudence, is a capital offence.

Theologians have always been ready to denounce those who believe differently from themselves as unbelievers. The great theologian and mystic al-Ghazālī (1059–1111) has a rather striking sentence in which he talks of theologians who recklessly hurl accusations of unbelief at those who differ from them, and call them unbelievers. This is called *takfīr*, pronouncing someone to be a *kāfir*, an unbeliever. They try, he says, 'to make paradise the benefice of a small clique of theologians'.[6] But such denunciations among theologians had little or no practical effect. The jurists were more latitudinarian than the theologians, and they did not pronounce *takfīr*, with its legal consequences, confiscation and death, without good reason.

Were there wars of religion between these different groups? There have been many intra-Islamic wars in Islamic history, and in some of them people on different sides professed different forms of Islam. But one cannot speak of wars of religion in the Islamic world in the sense that this term is used of the struggles in Europe in the sixteenth and seventeenth centuries. There were regional, tribal and dynastic wars with, shall we say, religious coloration. During the sixteenth century and for a while after, the sultans of Turkey and the shahs of Persia contended for the domination of the Middle East. The sultan was Sunnī; the shah was Shī'ite. Ottoman Shī'ites and Persian Sunnīs were therefore regarded by their rulers as potentially disloyal, and sometimes treated accordingly. But it would be an exaggeration to describe this as a Sunni-Shī'a war. There were other more or less religious struggles: rebellions by pseudo-Messiahs, outbreaks of violence from would-be reformers who came to purify Islam and change the world. But most of these were of brief duration and little effect. Some failed quickly and simply, by being defeated and crushed. Others achieved a more complex failure, by winning power, and then, with greater or less speed, reverting to the practices of those whom they had denounced and overthrown. The one great exception was the struggle between the Sunnī Abbasid caliphate of Baghdad and the Ismā'īlī Fatimid caliphate of Cairo in the high Middle Ages, and even that, before very long, became a clash of empires rather than of beliefs.

The disagreement between Sunnis and Shī'a has been likened to the split between Protestants and Catholics, an analogy that has meaning only in the very loose general sense of a large-scale division into two major religious camps. The main difference between Sunnis and Shī'a is not one of religious doctrine or authority. It was in origin a disagreement between parties on a political issue, about who should be the head of state, and by what right. The word Shī'a in Arabic means party and refers to the Shī'at 'Alī, those who believed that 'Alī as kinsman of the Prophet should be his successor as caliph and head of the community. The two groups developed along different lines, but the differences are primarily of experience, of emotion and attitudes rather than of doctrine or belief. Some have seen in Shi'ism a form of Persian national self-expression, even a Persian revolt against Sunni Arabism. This view, popular among European scholars at a time when racial theories were still influential in Western political thought, is far-fetched and untenable. For many centuries after the advent of Islam, Shi'ism had no ethnic or territorial label. It was brought to Iran, like Islam itself, by Arabs, and it would seem that most Persian Muslims were loyal Sunnis. But from the sixteenth century onwards, Shi'ism became the state religion of Iran which moreover was the only Shi'ite state of significance in the Islamic world. Not only was Iran a militant Shī'ite state; it was also surrounded on all sides by Sunni states – the Ottoman empire in the west, the Central Asian and Indian Sunni states to the east, and there was thus, inevitably, an interpenetration between Shī'ite religion and Iranian cultural and political self-awareness.

In general, the Muslim attitude to differences of belief and even of worship might be called latitudinarian. From time to time, especially in periods of domestic or external tension or conflict, there were attempts to define and impose an orthodoxy and to exclude all those who did not conform to it. But in general Muslims adhered to the principle laid down by a respected medieval theologian, for whom no one who prays towards Mecca can be considered an unbeliever.

The question of tolerance has acquired a new relevance in

our time. Generally speaking, in the Western world it is understood to mean the granting of rights, preferably equal rights, to people who are different. These rights include freedom of worship, freedom to organize, freedom to build and operate places of worship, and to differ from the majority or dominant religion, without loss of civil or political status. For Muslims tolerance has meant something quite different. The whole idea of tolerance is on both sides a fairly modern one, dating from after the great Wars of Religion in Europe, when both Protestants and Catholics finally decided that some kind of compromise, some sort of *modus vivendi* was necessary. In earlier times, full tolerance would not have been regarded as a virtue, but rather as a dereliction of duty – the obvious absurdity of giving the same rights to those who accept and those who reject the true faith. The proposition would be much the same whichever faith happened to be true.

Until the seventeenth century, there can be no doubt that, all in all, the treatment by Muslim governments and populations of those who believed otherwise was more tolerant and respectful than was normal in Europe. Islam has had its persecutions when, for one reason or another, Muslim governments or populations disobeyed the rules of their own holy law and denied the followers of the superseded religions even that measure of tolerance which the Holy Law assigns to them. But there is nothing in Islamic history to compare with the massacres and expulsions, the inquisitions and persecutions that Christians habitually inflicted on non-Christians and still more on each other. In the lands of Islam, persecution was the exception; in Christendom, sadly, it was often the norm.

The Reformation and the wars of religion brought a major change. From the seventeenth century onwards, the situation of non-Christians under Western Christian rule was no worse than that of the *dhimmīs* under Muslim rule and gradually became considerably better. Meanwhile, the deterioration in the status of the *dhimmī* was not only relative but also absolute. It is always difficult for the fortunate possessors of the Truth to tolerate the foolishness and contumacy of those who wilfully reject it and persist in their old errors. It is, however, easier when one's knowledge of one's own rightness is buttressed by overwhelming worldly power – the outward and visible sign of God's approval. Such tolerance becomes much more difficult when not Truth but Error enjoys the advantages of wealth and power, and when one's unbelieving compatriots and neighbours, no longer appropriately submissive, enjoy the support and encouragement of mighty, outside powers committed to various forms of unbelief. These powers, and their local acolytes, now challenged the supremacy of the believer, first in the world, then in his own country, finally even in his own home, where his previously assured authority was questioned by emancipated women and rebellious children, both misled by infidel ideas from abroad.

During the nineteenth and twentieth centuries, the old contract known as the *dhimma* broke down in most of the Muslim world. The Christian and to some extent even the Jewish subjects of the Muslim state, inspired by Western liberal ideas, were no longer satisfied with the assured but limited rights which it conferred. Muslim states and majorities, feeling themselves threatened, saw even the limited rights of the *dhimma* as a danger, and mistrusted the previously harmless domestic infidel as the agent and emissary of the more dangerous infidels abroad.

Over this period, the position of the non-Muslim subjects, on paper, improved greatly. Muslim governments, sometimes in response to foreign pressures, more often in response to imported foreign liberal and nationalist ideologies, gradually abandoned both the theory and practice of the *dhimma* and promulgated new laws and constitutions, according to which all subjects or, later, citizens, irrespective of religion, enjoyed equal status.

All too often, religious minorities were in fact worse off than before. The *dhimma* had given them a recognized legal status, established by no less an authority than the Holy Law, and accepted for centuries by the Muslim population as part of the divine social and political order. Under Ottoman rule, Christians and Jews were allowed not only to observe but even to enforce their own religious laws. Christian law, in all churches, prohibited both polygamy and concubinage. Rabbinic law, as interpreted in the Ottoman lands, permitted polygamy but not concubinage. Islamic law permitted both. Christian and Jewish religious authorities were able to try, condemn, sentence and punish members of their communities for disobeying these rules, even though such disobedience constituted no offence against the laws and ethos of the state and the dominant community. A Christian identity, under the sultan, involved submission to Christian as well as to sultanic authority.

The term second-class citizenship has a harsh sound to modern Western ears, but second-class citizenship – that is, some though not all of the rights of the citizen, recognized and respected – is better than no citizenship at all, and this last was very often the situation in which the religious minorities found themselves in the new dictatorships erected on the ruins of the democratic experiments. The classical Ottoman Empire enabled a multiplicity of religious and ethnic groups to live side by side in mutual tolerance and respect, subject only to the primacy of Islam and the supremacy of the Muslims. The liberal reformers and revolutionaries who abolished the old order and proclaimed the constitutional equality of all Ottoman citizens led the Ottoman Empire into the final bitter and bloody national struggles – the worst by far in the half-millennium of its history.

The Ottoman Empire has gone, but the issues posed in its final decades remain unresolved, and continue to trouble the political life of all the Ottoman successor states in the Balkans and the Middle East, as well as of other Muslim countries that have undergone parallel processes of development.

The Qur'ān, like other scriptures, provides a variety of guidance, and since the promulgation of that scripture, the range of choice has been further widened by the experience and interpretation of many generations in many lands. There is in Islam a tradition of unquestioning submission to authority. There is also a tradition of rebellion against authority perceived as unjust or illegitimate. Both traditions are firmly rooted in scripture and tradition; both were expanded and developed in theory and practice by subsequent generations of Muslims. In the same way, it is not difficult to find scriptural and juridical authority for both war and peace with the unbelievers. In the Qur'ān, the enemies of God are specified as the unbelievers, and they are doomed to hellfire (2:98; 41:19, 28). The believers are commanded to 'strike terror into God's enemy and your enemy'. But the struggle need not be to the death. 'If the enemy incline towards peace, do you also incline towards peace and trust in God.' (8:60–62) According to a striking passage, repeated several times in the Qur'an, 'if God had wished, He would have made all humankind one community' (11:118; 16:93; 42:8). But, by God's choice, the world is divided into different nations and religions, and God determines who shall embrace the truth and who shall go astray. And in this, surely, there is a powerful argument for compassion and tolerance.

NINE

Aspirations

Unlike India, China or Europe, the Middle East has no collective identity. The pattern, from the earliest times to the present day, has been one of diversity – in religion, in language, in culture, and above all in self-perception. The general adoption at the present time, in countries east and west and north and south of the so-called Middle East, and even in the Middle East itself, of this meaningless, colourless, shapeless, and for most of the world, inaccurate term is the best indication of the lack of a perceived common identity, either at home or abroad.

The four consecutive processes of Hellenization, Romanization, Christianization, and Islamization imposed some measure of unity on at least some parts of the region, and some elements of society in them. Islam, the first to embrace the whole region, the first to have its main centres of creativity and domination in the Middle East, gave the region the only common identity it has ever known. It is hardly surprising that those who seek something larger than tribal or factional or regional loyalties, something nobler than the existing state organisms, should respond to the appeal of Islam.

But there have been other appeals. For most of the twentieth century two ideas, both of European origin, dominated political thought and action in the Middle East – socialism and nationalism. By now both have been outdated, the one by its failure, the other by its success. For most Middle Easterners, socialism has been discredited by the collapse of its superpower sponsor, the Soviet Union and, more intimately, by the wretched performance of socialist regimes at home. Nationalism was not so much discredited as superseded. In all the countries of the region, now also including the former Soviet possessions, colonial domination has come to an end, and the coveted aim of sovereign independence has been attained. And this too has proved a bitter fruit.

In a few countries nationalism and socialism have been succeeded by their bastard offspring, national socialism – a term which might not unreasonably be applied to the one-party dictatorships that rule in Iraq and Syria. Like their central and south European predecessors and models, these too crawled out of the ruins of failed and collapsed democracies.

Democracy in the Western sense of the word – that is a political system in which freely contested elections are held at regular intervals and in which the government may be removed by the decision of the electorate, is rare in the Middle East. Many countries in the region hold elections – partly because this is the fashionable attire of the modern state, partly because some form of election is necessary to qualify for international aid and other benefits. But in most of these regimes, elections are changed by governments, not governments by elections. There are only two states in the region where genuine elections are held and governments can be – and sometimes are – changed by elections: Turkey and Israel.

The Israeli democracy has for long been something of an anomaly in the region. The state was founded by immigrants from Europe, and its European character was maintained and even accentuated by the Arab boycott which isolated the Jewish state from almost all forms of interaction with its neighbours. But this is changing. On the one hand, Jews of Middle Eastern and North African origin have become a majority of the Jewish population of Israel; on the other, the peace process, despite its many difficulties and reverses, has permeated the barriers. Israel now has treaty relations with two Arab countries and commercial relations with several others. Most important of all, it is intimately involved with the Palestinians, and this involvement, even in its most negative aspects, has alerted some Palestinian and other Arab observers to the merits of a liberal economy and polity. At the same time, these changes are affecting the very nature of Israeli identity and self-image, and the relative significance of faith, state and country.

Of far greater relevance to the experience, needs, and possibilities of the region is the example of Turkish democracy. At the beginning of the modern era, when the European empires began to expand into the Middle East, there were only two major powers, Turkey and Iran, in the region, and its history had been shaped for centuries past by their rivalry and the long series of wars fought between them. Throughout the period of European domination, Turkish and Iranian independence, though often endangered and attenuated, was never entirely lost. The Turks and the Iranians each had a capital and frontiers, however threatened; a government and state structure, however enfeebled. Both therefore had what a Westerner – though not at that time a Middle Easterner – might have called a sense of national identity, and with it a tradition of acceptance and allegiance among the people and of independent decision and action among the rulers. The founders of modern Turkey and Iran in the 1920s had to fight to retain their place in the comity of nations – but the place was there for them to retain. With the ending of foreign imperial domination, both resumed their inescapable role as the major powers of the region.

Today once again, as in the past, the two countries embody ideological choices – this time not between Sunni and Shī'a Islam, but between secular democracy and Islamic theocracy. Both are republican in form, both installed by charismatic leaders who overthrew the previous regimes. Kemal Atatürk established a secular democracy in place of the Sultan; the Ayatollah Khomeini founded an Islamic theocracy in place of the Shah. Their teachings and programs, Kemalism and Khomeinism, are seen by many as the two main alternative futures for the region.

Turkey is a reluctant candidate for any Middle Eastern role. In a country straddling the borders between the Middle East and Europe, the political and intellectual leadership of Turkey made a conscious choice for the West and for a Western identity. Once the scene of their greatest triumphs, the Middle East had become associated in their minds with decline, defeat and betrayal. The West, on the other hand, seemed to offer the means of economic development and of social and political liberation. The revolution of Kemal Atatürk, which ended the Ottoman sultanate and founded the Turkish republic, took major and decisive steps in this direction.

Secularism, as interpreted in the Turkish republic, did not mean the abandonment, still less the suppression, of their ancestral faith. It did mean a clear separation between religion and politics, between the Islamic clergy and the apparatus of government, and a shift of primary identity from community and religion to country and nation.

The other great change was the introduction of representative democracy. Many countries adopted the forms of constitutional and parliamentary government. These were always of limited effectiveness and often of brief duration. In Turkey, despite hard struggles and many setbacks, the development of democratic institutions continued. Today Turkey alone among the member states of the Organization of the Islamic Conference holds regular and free elections in which incumbent governments are sometimes defeated and relinquish power.

The Islamic revolution in Iran offers a different diagnosis of the ills of Middle Eastern society, and a different prescription for their cure. These depend on a different definition of the very character and identity of the patient. Like the French and Russian revolutions and unlike the various military and party coups d'état which have assumed the name and style of revolution in other parts of the region, what happened in Iran was a genuine revolution, expressing the anger and the aspirations of the great mass of the people and bringing about immense changes in every aspect of national life. Time will show whether these changes are for the better or for the worse.

Again like the French and Russian revolutions, the Iranian revolution evoked a powerful response in the world with which it shares a common universe of discourse – that is, the world of Islam. At first there was tremendous enthusiasm in all the Muslim lands, from West Africa to Southeast Asia, and in the diaspora. Since then, like the French and the Russians, the Iranian revolutionary leaders have antagonized much of their erstwhile following by their actions at home and abroad. But there are still many who are willing to excuse and even to imitate their sins for the sake of the ultimate dream of a just and pure society governed in accordance with the holy law of Islam.

There are increasing signs of strain within Iran, of growing disillusionment and even disaffection among a young population most of whom have grown to adulthood since the revolution. The unstoppable advance of modern communications – satellite television bringing revealing programs from the outside world, fax, internet and e-mail bringing messages of sedition – is augmenting this disaffection, which finds expression even in the limited freedom permitted to parliament and the media. Another sign of disillusionment is the growing attraction for the young of American popular culture – its music, its dress styles, and, in many subtle ways, its values. It was to this attraction that Khomeini alluded when he called America 'the Great Satan'. Satan, it will be remembered, is not a conqueror, not an exploiter. He is a tempter, a seducer, most dangerous when he smiles. As this disaffection grows and spreads, the regime responds with the classical weapons of an embattled autocracy – repression at home, terror and adventurism abroad. These will continue as long as the regime can count on the money from oil and the complicity or at least acquiescence of its foreign trading partners. If either of these supports falters, the regime will be in grave danger from its own people.

Neither side – democratic Turkey or fundamentalist Iran – is immune to the attractions of the other. In a general election held in Turkey in December 1995, a political party with an Islamic fundamentalist ideology won 21 per cent of the votes nationwide. Some of these may perhaps be counted as protest votes against the old parties. But what remains is a significant affirmation of support for the fundamentalist agenda, and for a while, the play of Turkey's multiparty politics enabled the fundamentalist leader to form and head a coalition with one of the secular parties. It was ended under pressure from the military, who see the preservation of the constitution and therefore of secularism as one of their principal duties. A fundamentalist religious opposition remains active both in parliament and in the country.

The Islamic Republic of Iran also has a written constitution and regular elections – both equally unknown to classical Islamic precept or practice. Elections are contested and the political debate is sometimes lively. But the limits are narrowly defined and do not permit any questioning of the Islamic basis of government. All candidates are examined by a religious council, and barred from competing if they do not meet its requirements. There is therefore no way of knowing what percentage of the Iranian electorate would vote for a secular party or programme if they were given the chance. The indications are that it would be considerable. Perhaps for that very reason the opportunity to express that choice is not allowed to them. But the tension is palpable, and it seems that Iran, like Turkey but differently, embodies both choices, one in power, the other in opposition.

An important difference between the two sides is in their self-image and self-projection. The rulers of Iran see themselves as the leaders of world Islam, of a movement for Muslim self-renewal and the restoration of Muslim greatness and glory. To this end they encourage and promote radical Muslim movements all over the Muslim world and among Muslim minorities in Europe, America, and elsewhere. This encouragement takes the form of money and infrastructure, weapons and training, and often of strategic direction. The Turks have no such program but aim at the more modest objective of preserving their troubled and embattled democracy from its internal and external enemies. Turkey sees itself as a nation-state, its identity defined by language, culture, institutions, and, most basic of all, by country. It does not offer itself as model or example to others, nor – apart from some help to the Turkic republics of Central Asia – does it provide material or moral aid to supporters elsewhere. Yet the Turkish model is not without impact. Twice before the Turks have offered leadership to the region – under the Ottoman sultans in Islamic *jihad*, under Kemal Atatürk in national self-liberation. They may do so again.

There are already signs of change in several Arab countries. These still fall short of democracy in the sense in which that word is used in Europe and America, but they represent a considerable improvement on the forms of government familiar in their own past and in their neighbours' present. Such Western notions as human rights and political participation have been increasingly discussed; such traditional Islamic values as dignity and consultation have been given new meaning. Cautious moves towards democratization may be seen in Jordan, Egypt and, to a somewhat lesser extent, in some of the Gulf States. A few countries now hold elections which may be contested by opposition candidates. There is as yet no Arab country in which the government may be changed by means of an election, but an increasing measure of opposition, and with it of freedom of expression, is being permitted. Elections of a sort are held in many other countries, but usually they are no more than a ceremonial recognition of the political facts – the equivalent of a British coronation or American inauguration, not of a British or American election. The opposite extremes are reflected in 1996 elections organized by the Lebanese government and the Palestine authority. The former, because of local circumstances, was a prearranged ceremony. The latter, again because of local circumstances, was probably the freest and fairest election held in the Arab world.

The process of democratization is not limited to the holding of elections. There is a growing freedom of debate in a few countries and more especially in the increasingly important expatriate Arabic media. These, though published for the most part in London or Paris, have both contributors and readers in Arab countries.

Democracy in its western form is making progress among the Arabs. So too, is Islamic fundamentalism. In one country, the Sudan, the fundamentalists have seized power, and are using it to wage a *jihad* against the Christian and animist south. In Afghanistan a religious movement – Sunni and anti-Iranian but profoundly fundamentalist – already controls much of the country. In others, notably Algeria and to a lesser extent Egypt and the kingdoms and principalities of Arabia, fundamentalists seek by terror and other means to overthrow and replace the existing governments. In Syria they are bloodily suppressed. In Jordan and Morocco they have been in some measure co-opted into the political process. In virtually all these countries fundamentalism is a powerful force, its appeal becoming stronger as disillusionment grows with the existing regimes. It is by no means impossible that fundamentalist regimes may emerge or seize power in other Arab countries. Those with oil may survive the transition. Those with no oil revenues to cushion the rigours of fundamentalist policies will have a harder time.

Among the score or so of countries that constitute the Arab world, a common pattern is emerging in which loyalty is claimed and given at three levels – interacting, sometimes in harmony, sometimes in conflict. The lowest level might, for want of a better term, be called 'local'. This may be tribal, ethnic, or exceptionally, national – that is to say, a group held together by a sense of common descent, real or imagined (whether it is in fact real or imagined is of no consequence; it is the conviction of common descent that matters), and thus defining itself against others. Such are the many tribal and clan distinctions among the Arabs themselves. Such too are the tribal and ethnic distinctions that split the only significant ethnic minorities in the Arab world, that is to say, the Berbers in North Africa, the Kurds in the Near East, and – a different and diverse group – the blacks in Mauritania and the Sudan.

Sometimes the bond may be sectarian or religious – membership of a particular religious community or of a subgroup within that community. Christians in Lebanon are sub-divided into Orthodox, Catholic and various smaller groups, and these in turn are further sub-divided by clan, family or faction. Sometimes the bond may be regional – related to a place, a district or a province. Or, of course, it may be any combination of these.

Such regional, sectarian or tribal entities may shape or even dominate the political life of a country by providing the necessary solidarity which enables a group to seize and retain power. In Iraq, for example, the regime has rested largely on people coming from one particular place, the town of Takrīt. Syria offers a somewhat different pattern – an ascendancy which is both regional and sectarian, that of the Alawis from the northwest. In the Yemen, we see struggles among three rival Muslim denominations as well as tribal and regional conflicts.

Above the local level is what one might call the intermediate level – that of the sovereign state. Most of these are new, with new frontiers and sometimes even new identities. Some of these were based on genuine historical entities; others were entirely artificial.

The third and highest level transcends the sovereign state and expresses the aspiration towards some greater unity, something more dignified and more honourable than the often rather grubby domestic politics of some of the existing states. These larger entities are conceived either in national terms – pan-Turkism, pan-Arabism, pan-Iranism – or in religious terms. For this last, there is only one candidate, pan-Islam, though it has been interpreted in very different ways.

At the present time, the trans-territorial nationalist movements seem to command little support. Pan-Iranism was never much of a force. Outside Iran, there are only two Persian-speaking populations of any size – in the former Soviet republic of Tajikistan, and in part of Afghanistan. Neither shows much interest, and both are predominantly Sunni, a factor of some importance, especially with the present rulers of Iran, for whom the divisive power of religion is far greater than the unifying power of language. Pan-Turkism, an impossible dream as long as imperial Russia maintained its grip on its Turkic populations, enjoyed a window of opportunity when, in the wake of the Bolshevik Revolution, the Russian Empire faltered and fell apart. That window was closed when the Soviet regime consolidated its hold over the former imperial territories. The break-up of the Soviet Union has not so far led to a resurgence of pan-Turkism, though cultural and economic links between the Turkish-speaking states have been restored and will probably increase.

Pan-Arabism, as an aspiration, was by far the most potent of the three, and for long was a sacrosanct ideological principle in all the Arab countries, some of which even incorporated it in their constitutions. But as the various Arab states established themselves more firmly and defined and pursued their various national interests with growing clarity, their commitment to pan-Arabism became more and more perfunctory. At the present time, after a series of bitter inter-Arab conflicts, even the customary lip service is often lacking. It may be that at some future time pan-Arabism will return. For the moment, the Arab world remains a mosaic of separate nation states, linked by language, culture, religion and history, but not forming a political bloc and with no real desire for a closer union.

Pan-Islam has proved more durable, though it is still far from triumphant. Among many varieties, two trends have predominated. One is political in inspiration, sometimes diplomatic in method, and usually conservative in policy. The other is popular, usually radical, often subversive. Both at times enjoy governmental support, the one by patriarchal, the other by revolutionary regimes. Both also receive significant financial support from private individuals, mainly in Arabia and the Gulf, who combine new wealth with old aspirations. There is of course no clear differentiation, since governments try to exploit popular movements elsewhere, while popular movements seek to influence or even control government. Though both kinds have so far had only limited success, the level of religious involvement in both national and international politics – and thus in political self-identification – is far greater than in other communions. On the whole, however, diplomatic pan-Islamism has proved, at best, inconclusive, and the attempts, from time to time, by some Muslim governments to make Islam an organizing principle of international relations have had little effect.

Popular, radical Islam is another matter. The current wave of religious militancy, one of many in Islamic history, has not yet crested, and it may well engulf more Muslim countries before its force is spent. But if the policies of Iran and Sudan, the two countries where Islamic revolutionaries have won power, are any guide, Islamic states will be no less insistent than their predecessors on their statehood – each state with its own structures and interests, elites and allegiances, its own identity and will to survive.

In September, 1862, Âli Pasha, at that time Foreign Minister of the Ottoman Empire, wrote a letter to his ambassador in Paris in which he gave what diplomats call a 'tour d'horizon'. He surveyed the diplomatic situation in Europe generally, country by country, and ended with Italy, at that time in the throes of the struggle for national unification. Âli Pasha wrote in his letter:

> Italy, which is inhabited only by a single race, speaking the same language and professing the same religion, experiences so many difficulties in its unification. And for the moment, all it has achieved is anarchy and disorder. Judge what would happen in Turkey if free scope were given to all the different national aspirations ... It would need a century and torrents of blood to establish a fairly stable state of affairs.[7]

Ali Pasha was a true prophet – indeed he was rather better at foreseeing the future than at seeing the present. Already in his day, these ideas, which he feared with good reason, were entering the Ottoman lands, and beginning their work of disruption. Since then more than a century has passed; the blood still flows, and even a 'fairly stable state of affairs' has not yet been attained. All these states, whatever their real shape or self-image, are being changed, at different speeds and in different ways, by modernization, bringing with it wider literacy, the information revolution, and the long delayed emancipation and participation of women. All this is affecting, and will ultimately transform, the ways in which their peoples see themselves and others, and may even lead to the emergence of open and free societies. But this will take time, and meanwhile they are tormented by the interaction of multiple and often conflicted identities.

⟝REFERENCES

1 Ibn Khaldūn, *Muqaddima*, ed. E. Quatremère, Paris, 1858, vol. I, p. 237.
2 Ibn Khaldūn, *Kitāb al-ʿIbar*, Bulaq 1284/1867, vol. v, p. 371.
3 *Turkey and the Crimean War*, London, 1862, p. 32.
4 cited in Mahmud Kemal Inal, *Osmanli Devrinde Son Sadriazamlar*, Istanbul, 1940–1953, p. 1892.
5 Rudi Paret, 'Sure 2,256: lā ikrāha fi d-dīni. Toleranz oder Resignation?', *Der Islam*, 45, (1969), pp. 299–300.
6 Abū Muhammad al-Ghazālī, *Faysal al-tafriqa bayn al-Islam wa'l-Zandaqa*, Cairo, 1901, p. 68.
7 ed. M. Cavid Baysun, 'Ali Paşa'nın Fransızca bir mektubu.' in *Tarih Dergisi*, 5, 1953, p. 144.

⹀FURTHER READING

The literature on nationalist, religious and related movements in the Middle East is enormous and is for the most part readily accessible. The following suggestions for further reading include some important recent publications, as well as some earlier specialized studies that I have found particularly relevant.

Fouad Ajami, *The Dream Palace of the Arabs, a Generation's Odyssey*, New York, 1998.

Bozkurt Güvenç, 'Secular Trends and Turkish Identity', in *Perceptions: Journal of International Affairs*, ii (1997–8), pp. 46–72.

Ulrich W. Haarmann, 'Ideology and history, identity and alterity: the Arab image of the Turk from the 'Abbasids to modern Egypt', in *International Journal of Middle East Studies*, 20 (1988), pp. 175–196.

Idem, 'Glaubensvolk und Nation im islamischen und lateinischen Mittelalter', in Berlin-Brandenburgische Akademie der Wissenschaften, *Berichte und Abhandlungen*, 2, Berlin, 1996, pp. 161–199.

Riva Kastoryano, *La France, l'Allemagne et leurs immigrés: négocier l'identité*, Paris, 1996.

Alberto Melloni and Gianni La Bella (eds), *L'Alterità: Concezioni ed esperienze nel cristianesimo contemporaneo*, Bologna, 1995.

Krzystof Michalski, (ed.), *Identität im Wandel*, Stuttgart, 1995.

Krzystof Michalski, (ed.), *Identität im Wandel*, Stuttgart, 1995.

Patrik von zur Mühlen, *Zwischen Hakenkreuz und Sowjetstern: Der Nationalismus der sowjetischen Orientvölker im Zweiten Weltkrieg*, Düsseldorf, 1971.

Franz Rosenthal, 'The Stranger in Medieval Islam', in *Arabica*, 44 (1997), pp. 35–75.

Lucetta Scaraffia, *Rinnegati: per una storia dell'identità occidentale*, Rome-Bari, 1993.

Yael Zerubavel, *Recovered Roots: Collective Memory and the Making of Israeli National Tradition*, Chicago & London, 1995.

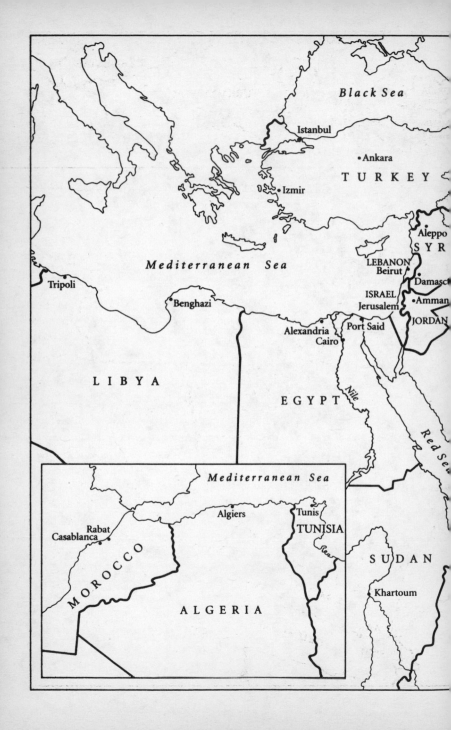

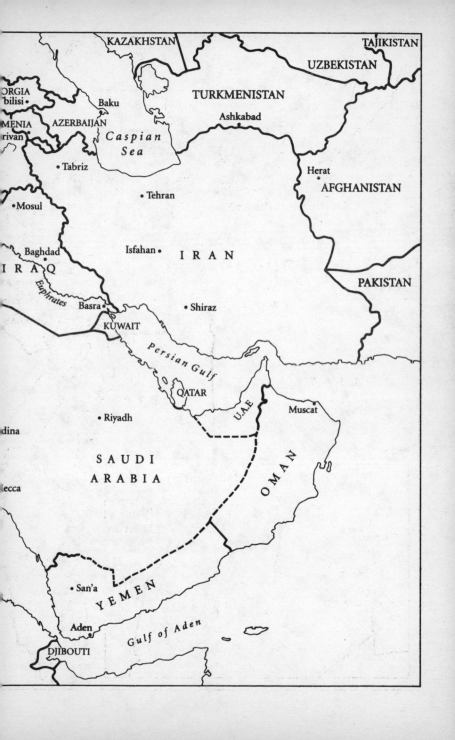

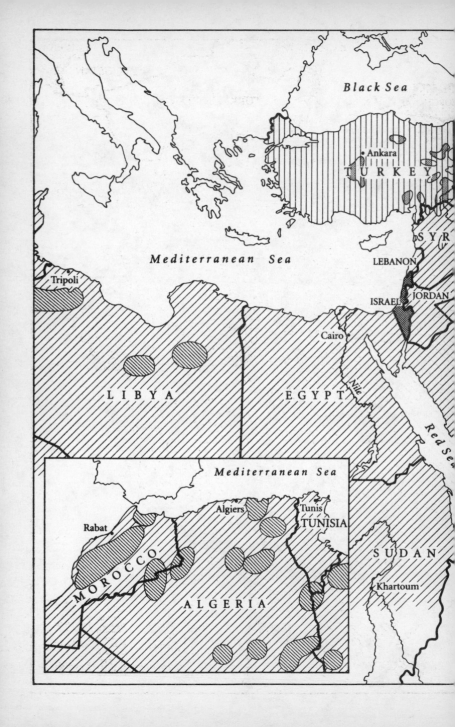

Black Sea

Ankara

T U R K E Y

S Y R

LEBANON

Mediterranean Sea

Tripoli

ISRAEL

JORDAN

Cairo

L I B Y A

E G Y P T

Nile

Red Sea

Mediterranean Sea

Algiers

Tunis

TUNISIA

Rabat

M O R O C C O

A L G E R I A

S U D A N

Khartoum

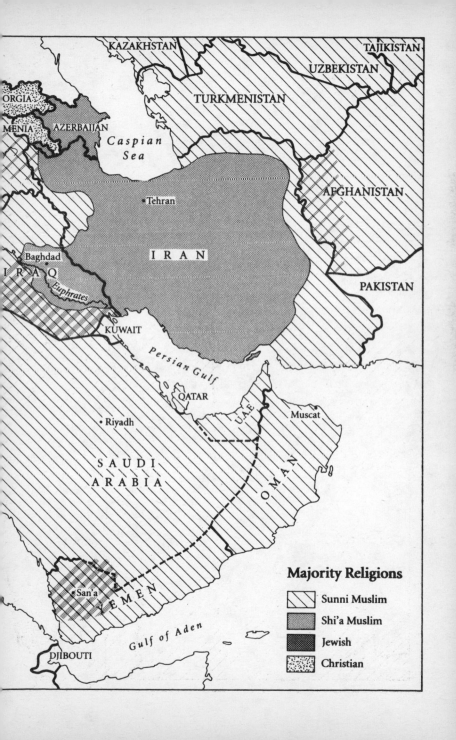

Majority Religions

Sunni Muslim
Shi'a Muslim
Jewish
Christian

INDEX